# VALLEY OF THE
# GOLDEN MUMMIES

# VALLEY

# GOLDEN

*Virgin*

# OF THE
# MUMMIES

ZAHI HAWASS

*Editor:* BARBARA BURN

*Designer:* ANA ROGERS

*Principal photographers:* MARC DEVILLE, KENNETH GARRETT, GUY MIDKIFF, and PHILIPPE PLAILLY

First published in Great Britain in 2000 by
Virgin Publishing Ltd
Thames Wharf Studios
Rainville Road
London
W6 9HA

A catalogue record for this book is available from the British Library.

ISBN 1 85227 849 8

First published in 2000 by Harry N. Abrams, Inc., New York

Printed and bound in Japan

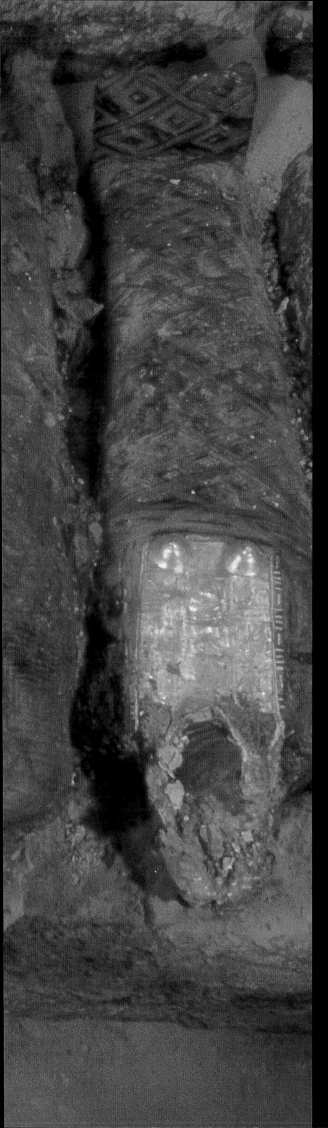

# CONTENTS

# INTRODUCTION

WHEN I GRADUATED FROM HIGH SCHOOL AT THE AGE OF FIFTEEN AND A HALF in the small village of Abeedia in Damietta, I dreamed of becoming a lawyer, but what I learned during my very first week at Alexandria University, when I started reading law books, was that this was not at all what I wanted. Disheartened, I went to the Faculty of Arts, where they told me a new archaeology department with a good future had just opened. The year was 1963. At that time, very few people knew that digging for ancient ruins and artifacts was a recognized discipline. I liked the idea, so for four years I studied archaeology, art, and ancient languages, concentrating on the Greco-Roman Period. But most of my interest was focused on campus politics. I was elected president of the student union and spent much of my time involved in social activities. When I completed my studies and joined the Antiquities Department in Cairo in 1968, I therefore experienced quite a shock.

The head of the department, the late Dr. Gamal Mokhtar, later a close friend, assigned me to the position of Antiquities Inspector at Tuna el-Gebel, a remote site in Middle Egypt located west of the famous ancient capital of El Amarna. At the age of twenty-one, I did not want to live in the middle of nowhere, but, when I looked around at the glum faces of senior archaeologists in the department doing the paperwork required of any government official, staying in Cairo did not look like an appealing alternative. To make matters worse, when a young woman I was dating asked me about my job and I told her I was an archaeologist, she burst out laughing. I constantly found myself having to explain what an archaeologist was to people who did not understand. So I decided to quit my job and become a diplomat instead.

For six months I bought books on politics and economics and studied hard in an effort to join the Ministry of Foreign Affairs, but they chose only three candidates out of many and I was not one of them. When I returned to the Antiquities Department, I was called in to meet with Dr. Mokhtar. He asked why I had not gone to Tuna el-Gebel, and I told him that I could not live in the desert. He replied that if I did not go to the site, he would issue an official decree banning me from the department forever. So I left Cairo for Tuna el-Gebel soon afterward, very angry and anxious about what I could possibly do and whom I could possibly meet in the unknown world of the Middle Egyptian desert.

As I excavated at this site and then later at Kom Abu-Bellou in Lower Egypt, I began to develop an affinity for the day-to-day work of archaeology, which combines hands-on physical activity and the management of people with the excitement of making discoveries. Before long, I could hear the words inside me—"I have found my real love"—and since then, I have dedicated my life to this work. I like to tell my story to young people who are unsure of their direction or who want to be doctors or lawyers just because of what they see in the movies. There is potential inside us that we cannot even imagine, and if we give ourselves completely to something, it will give us a lot in return.

*Page 10:* The Great Sphinx and the Pyramids of Giza at sunset

*Below:* The author (first row at right) with his fellow students at Alexandria University in 1965

*Bottom:* The author (left), in 1981, discusses the future of the monuments at Tuna el-Gebel with the late Kamal el-Mallakh, who discovered the solar boat of Khufu at Giza.

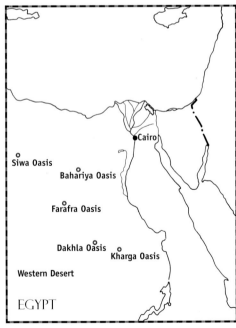

**The Western Desert**

*Top left:* The author at Abdydos in 1969

In 1976 I was working at Abu Simbel, the Nubian site of the well-known temples of Ramses II, when I read in the newspaper that thieves had broken through a wall of the big storage house in Giza and walked off with dozens of artifacts. Dr. Mokhtar suggested to General Auda Ahmed Auda that I be called in from Abu Simbel because he knew of my administrative abilities and believed I could make sure this would never happen again. One month later, we caught all the thieves, and the artifacts were returned; the thieves are still in jail today. That is how I came to be Inspector of the Pyramids at Giza.

The author in the desert of Yemen in 1977

In 1977 Bahariya Oasis was put under the same jurisdiction as the Giza monuments, so I went to visit the sites there for the first time with four colleagues. It is funny to think back and realize we were all standing on what would be one of the most exciting archaeological sites of the new millennium, and we were not even aware of it. Had we known what lay beneath our feet we might have stayed there and not gone in all different directions. Atef Hassan left archaeology to become a tour guide; Wafaa El Sediek now lives in Germany; Samia El Mallah got her doctorate and now works at the Egyptian Museum in Cairo; and Mirvat Ramadan still works at Giza.

We stayed for two days in the main village of El Bawiti in a shabby, unfurnished resthouse, because there were no hotels or telephones in the area. I met with the Chief of the Antiquities Guards, Sheikh Aiady Ahmed Soliman, who had only five employees. I realized then that this was a virgin site and I very much liked the kind people of the Oasis, but it never crossed my mind that I might someday excavate there. In fact, I recall that Mirvat Ramadan told me she felt sure I would excavate in Bahariya someday and that I laughed at the idea. I was just starting my work at the pyramids, and I could not imagine that anything in the Oasis could compare with the excitement of Giza. I was concerned, however, with protecting and conserving the existing sites with only six guards and no Antiquities Inspector. I saw that the paintings in the Twenty-sixth Dynasty tomb of Bannantiu were in need of consolidation before they completely deteriorated, as was the cartouche containing the name of Alexander the Great at his temple. But no one was willing to come from Cairo to live in this remote region.

Then someone in the village told me that a young man from Bahariya, Ashry Shaker, was a first-year student in archaeology in Cairo, and I figured that he might eventually make it possible for us to open a new office in the Oasis. I returned to Bahariya in 1980 to see about renting an office there, but I was not given any funds to support the venture. I recommended Shaker to the Antiquities Department, and then I accepted a Fulbright Fellowship to obtain my master's degree and a doctorate in Egyptology at the University of Pennsylvania. When I returned to Egypt in 1987, the department had appointed Ashry Shaker as Antiquities Inspector of Bahariya, and I was made Director General of Giza, Saqqara, Imbaba, and Bahariya Oasis.

The author in his office at Giza at the time he was made Inspector of the Pyramids in 1978

A unique tomb in the upper level of the Tombs of the Pyramid Builders

*Below:* The lower level of the Tombs of the Pyramid Builders, southeast of the Giza Pyramids

I began by concentrating all my excavations at the Giza Pyramids, where I discovered the Tombs of the Officials and the Tombs of the Pyramid Builders. My only involvement in Bahariya was to increase the number of guards and inspectors at the sites and to establish a conservation laboratory. I visited the area only two more times with students from Cairo University before the discovery in 1996 that changed my life and the future of Bahariya.

We did not announce the discovery, however, until three years later. After preliminary work was done at the site, we reburied the tombs to prevent looters from plundering the treasure and to protect them, because there was no budget or staff to launch a full-scale excavation in 1996. But it was important that we establish a plan for long-term conservation. My first priority is always conservation and restoration. New excavations are exciting, but they can wait, because the sand will continue to preserve a buried site, but if you do not conserve what you have already discovered, then you lose history.

The year 1999 was a good one for me, one in which all my work over the years began to bear fruit. The restoration work on the Great Sphinx, which we had begun in 1988, was finally completed, and I was presented with the First Class Award of Arts and Sciences by President Hosni Mubarak. We uncovered the symbolic tomb of Osiris beneath the causeway of the second pyramid of Khafre, and we showed it, along with the latest excavations at Giza live, on Fox Television in March. At the same time, I faced several difficulties, especially those caused by the ridiculous rumors posted on the Internet about my hiding evidence of lost civilizations and going through a secret tunnel from my bathroom to chambers beneath the pyramids! These allegations had not been made by archaeologists or Egyptologists but by people with various theories about the pyramids, and it was frustrating and time-consuming to refute the accusations and deal with people who insisted that they be given access to the historic

The author inspects his excavation site at Saqqara in 1998.

sites. Because of the fragility of these sites, we cannot allow everyone with a theory to conduct research there unless they are affiliated with a scientific institution or museum. In order to keep the general public informed, I began my own Web site at *guardians.net/hawass* to post accurate and up-to-date data about our excavations.

It was at this time that I chose to go to Bahariya, not only because it would be a welcome break from all the people who were hounding me at my office, but because we were eager to see what needed to be done at the Valley of the Golden Mummies. The team that I chose for the excavation included several people who work with me on the Giza Plateau: archaeologists Mahmoud Afifi, Mansour Boriak, Tarek el-Awady, and Aiman Wahby; conservators Nasry Iskander and Moustafa Abdul Qader; architects Abdul Hamied Kotb and Hamdi Rashwan; electrical engineer Mahmoud Helmy; and epigrapher Noha Abdul Hafiz. Two weeks before we were to leave, I had dinner with my friends Lisa Truitt, a National Geographic Society producer, and her husband, Doug, a *New York Times* correspondent, who both live in Cairo, together with our mutual friend Abdul Raof El Reedy, Egypt's former Ambassador to the United States, and his wife, Fareeda. When I told them I was preparing to leave for the Valley of the Golden Mummies, Lisa asked if she could film our first excavation there. She had produced the highly successful IMAX film *Mysteries of Egypt*, narrated by Omar Sharif, with which I was very impressed, so I accepted the idea and was happy to hear that the talented National Geographic photographer Kenneth Garrett would join us.

Since we began excavating in March 1999, we have uncovered 105 complete mummies at Bahariya and numerous skeletal remains. Never before has such a large number of perfectly preserved mummies been found in Egypt. This unique group, which dates to the Greco-Roman Period, exhibits a variety of styles and social status, and some are lavishly gilded from head to chest, reminiscent of the burial of Tutankhamun. Considering the rate at which graves have been robbed since ancient times, right up to the present day, it is remarkable that such a pristine site can still be found undisturbed. I estimate that the entire cemetery, which may cover nearly four square miles, will contain up to ten thousand mummies and take fifty years to excavate.

Archaeology is a painstakingly slow scientific process, not usually the subject of media attention, but the moment we announced this discovery in June 1999, the Valley of the

Golden Mummies—named for the depression in which they were buried within the Oasis—attained international fame virtually overnight. The gilded faces of the mummies have been seen on magazine covers from Italy to Japan, and the discovery has been celebrated in all the archaeology magazines and on the front pages of the *Los Angeles Times* and the *New York Times.* The site was also featured in many other American and European publications, including *Newsweek, U.S. News and World Report, Le Figaro,* and the *National Geographic,* as well as in Lisa Truitt's television documentary.

Mummies inspire both terror and awe in people, probably because they seem to be connected with a world beyond our own. I have worked around the pyramids for twenty years, making important discoveries about the pyramid builders and working-class Egyptians, but now when I deliver a lecture, people only want to hear about the golden mummies. Indeed, 1999 might as well have been called the Year of the Mummy. At least three major books on mummies were published during 1998 and 1999, and the popularity of the recent motion picture *The Mummy* attests to a widespread fascination with the subject. We seem to be experiencing a resurgence of interest in mummies not seen since the turn of the nineteenth century, when the dead were taken out of Egypt by the thousands for scientific research and sold as medicinal remedies or ghoulish novelty items to unwrap at parties.

Before this discovery at Bahariya Oasis, the study of mummies had not been my particular field of interest (as it is for some archaeologists), nor was Greco-Roman archaeology,

**The author (center) with his team at the Valley of the Golden Mummies**

although the latter was my major area of study as an undergraduate. I love my work at the pyramids in large part because I am learning about the common people, that 80 percent of the ancient Egyptians about whom we know so much less than we do about ancient royalty. But I have to admit that the Oasis site—and what it may have to tell—has come to thrill me.

I cannot account for the mass appeal of the golden mummies, but as a scholar I can say that the Bahariya mummies are more than just beautiful faces. In spite of their profound silence, they may help us answer a wide range of historical questions: How did the people of Bahariya Oasis, who had been greatly influenced by pharaonic culture for centuries before Alexander's conquest of Egypt in 332 B.C., respond and react to the imposition of Greek, and later Roman, rule during a period that lasted until A.D. 642? Was the political and economic transformation tumultuous? What was daily life like for the people of the Oasis at different periods? What types of diseases did they suffer? How and at what rate did the mythology and religious practices of pharaonic Egypt change and eventually disappear? We are only just beginning to answer some of these questions, thanks to this discovery, which begins a new era of archaeology for Bahariya Oasis, practically a virgin site until now. I believe Bahariya will prove to be the richest excavation site in Egypt for Egyptian, Greek, and Roman scholars alike. It is certainly the newest and most extensive source of information, and it will provide us for years to come with a more thorough understanding of life in Egypt from the Middle Kingdom onward.

This Oasis contains a wide range of monuments, tombs, and temples dating from as early as the Eighteenth Dynasty through the Greco-Roman and Coptic Periods. Several of these sites were discovered and partially or completely excavated by earlier archaeologists, but then abandoned and buried again over the ages. I include in this book descriptions of all the significant sites of Bahariya because very few people—members of the general public and scholars alike—know much about the exciting discoveries that have been made there. Part I is dedicated to the Valley of the Golden Mummies—its discovery and excavation, a description of the mummies and artifacts found in the tombs in light of what they can tell us about the economic, social, and religious life of the people of the Oasis during the Greco-Roman Period. Part II summarizes the history of Bahariya Oasis up to the present day and surveys the religious beliefs and mummification practices of ancient Egypt from the Predynastic Period through the fourth century A.D. In Part III, I describe in detail other sites in the Oasis, especially the Roman settlement at El Haiz, and a number near El Bawiti that have been recently opened to the public or that are slated for further excavation. I end the book with a tantalizing glimpse of some of the other new tombs we are in the process of uncovering.

My personal belief is that mummies should not be displayed for sensational reasons, but we did decide to remove five of the most beautiful examples to the new museum in Bahariya. This will enable scholars to study them and allow tourists to view some of the wonders from the cemetery, which we cannot open to the public while it is an active excavation site. This book, however, will enable me to share the beauty and adventure of finding such wealth from our past without exposing the mummies to the risks posed by tourist traffic. My hope is to

educate everyone, especially Egyptians, about our history and heritage so that we may be able to learn something from it for our own future. I believe the most important reason we dig in the dirt, often from sunrise to sunset, is to figure out not only how people used to live but also how we can learn from how they lived to live better ourselves.

Behind every archaeological site are countless good stories—those that the artifacts reveal about the past and those that arise from the people currently living and working in the area under study. Archaeologists who are concerned only with artifacts can get lost in the details and miss the significance of why we do what we do. The discipline of archaeology developed as a window into our past, but I think the people who inhabit our areas of excavation today are just as important as the ancients, so I have included both in the scope of this book. Let me take you then on a journey to the Oasis in the desert to smell the perfume of thousands of years and to discover the secrets that lie hidden beneath the sand.

**A farmer carries in greens from the field to feed his animals at the end of the day.**

# PART I
# VALLEY OF THE GOLDEN MUMMIES

# A DONKEY'S TALE: THE DISCOVERY

On March 2, 1996, I walked into the Antiquities Department tent next to the excavation of the Tombs of the Pyramid Builders, which are located southeast of the Great Sphinx at Giza, and found my assistant Mansour Boriak imitating me in front of some members of our excavation team. He was unaware that I had come up behind him until he heard me laugh, and then he almost fainted. A senior archaeologist and my favorite colleague at Giza, Mansour reports to me regularly about the status of other sites within my jurisdiction, but he loves to make up stories about discoveries or problems and then fool me into believing them. This time I enjoyed turning the tables by pretending to be very upset as I walked out of the tent in a huff. So when Mansour came into my office later that day saying excitedly, "Doctor! Doctor! Ashry Shaker is here. Something very important has been discovered in Bahariya Oasis!" I was sure it was another of his pranks and I proceeded to ignore him.

"No, sir. This time it is true. Something very exciting was found," he said with an impish smile. But I did not believe him until Ashry Shaker, director of the Antiquities Department office at Bahariya Oasis, was standing in front of me with his typically serious expression. Ashry is a polite man with a beard and a moustache, a man you can trust. He reported that an Antiquities Guard at the Temple of Alexander the Great had been riding his donkey in the desert when the donkey's leg fell into a hole. When Ashry realized that the hole was an opening to a tomb, he rushed to Giza to tell me about this very important discovery and to convince me to come to Bahariya right away. When I asked Ashry what made him so sure this was truly important, he said, "I followed the guard to the site and had a look myself. Inside I saw part of the face of a mummy sticking out of the sand. It appears to be shiny, like gold."

At this time, my own active excavation sites included most of the ongoing digs at the Giza Plateau and a site in Saqqara near the pyramid of Teti, the first Sixth Dynasty king of the Old Kingdom. Because I could not be at each site for which I was responsible, I instructed Ashry to appoint an inspector to begin excavating the site at Bahariya and told him I would come down as soon as possible.

I drove to Bahariya Oasis one week after receiving the exciting news about the new discovery of the mysterious hole in the ground near the Temple of Alexander the Great. What used to take the ancients four days by camel took me only three hours by jeep, traveling southwest along the ancient trade route for more than 260 miles by desert road, where one sees only endless stretches of sand that reveal no hint of what may lie beneath. When I arrived in the village of El Bawiti, which is in the center of the Oasis close to the site of El Qasr, its

Antiquities Guard Abdul Maugoud and his donkey, who first discovered the hole in the desert that led archaeologists to the Valley of the Golden Mummies

*Pages 20–21:* Sunrise over the Valley of the Golden Mummies

*Page 22:* Poles set up by the archaeological team around the outer borders of the cemetery indicate that it may be as large as four square miles.

ancient capital, Ashry Shaker introduced me to Abdul Maugoud, a very serious man of forty-four whose donkey had literally stumbled upon the tomb.

For ten years, six days a week, eight hours a day, Abdul Maugoud has stood in the doorway of the Temple of Alexander the Great—the same door that ancient worshipers passed through to make offerings to their gods. His job is to make sure that no one enters or violates the surrounding area. To protect himself from the intense sun, he always wears the traditional dress of men in the Oasis, a long white cotton robe, or *gallabia*, and a white scarf, or *ema*, around his head. I said to him, "Tell me, Sheikh Abdul Maugoud, tell me what happened."

Abdul Maugoud clasped his hands together in front of him and never looked at me, keeping his eyes on the sand as a sign of respect as he began his story. The guard who usually replaces him had been late on the afternoon of March 1, so Abdul Maugoud waited by the temple door for half an hour. Suddenly he noticed his donkey running toward the desert, holding in its mouth one end of the rope that usually hangs from each side of its head. This was an unusual sight, because donkeys do not often run unless they are forced to do so. Also, they normally bray when these steering devices are used and do not willingly take the rope into their own mouths. Abdul Maugoud ran after the donkey, but it went too far and he turned back, not wanting to leave the temple unguarded for very long. From the top of the hill on which the temple stands, he could see that his ride home had stopped almost a mile away, but he could not tell why. After another hour and a half, the replacement guard finally arrived, apologizing profusely for being so late. Abdul Maugoud told him to take his staff

A section of the Greco-Roman cemetery that is not yet excavated

and fetch the runaway donkey, but they saw that it was on its way back. Eventually the animal stopped in front of Abdul Maugoud with the rope still in its mouth. He got on, but the donkey refused to take the same desert road they had used to go home every working day for the last ten years, so he dismounted and tried to push the animal, but it continued to balk. It seemed determined to go back toward the desert. The other guard thought that the donkey was trying to tell Abdul Maugoud something and that he should follow the animal to see what its story was.

The bewildered man got back on, and the donkey took him to the spot where it had stopped earlier. Suddenly it turned its head and grabbed the rope from Abdul Maugoud's hand, nearly causing him to fall off. He saw that the donkey had dropped the rope in front of a hole in the ground, so he got off, knelt down, and looked into the hole. He could hardly believe his eyes. He went immediately to Ashry Shaker's office and told him there was something shining under the sand.

New sites such as the Valley of the Golden Mummies in Bahariya are rare. For the most part, important archaeological sites have long been established, and excavation—and in most cases preservation—is an ongoing process. This episode demonstrates that, as in most sciences, regardless of how carefully we carry out our research and planning, some of our best work is the result of pure luck. Minor archaeological finds can occur on a daily basis in Egypt, but it is not unusual for even a major discovery to be followed by months during which nothing is

**The northern borders of the Valley of the Golden Mummies**

unearthed. Of course, this is largely because of the restricted digging seasons, which take place during the month of November and then again from January through March or even later, the length of time depending on many things, such as weather, budget, and other obligations. An archaeological team often works from dawn until dusk, and real work is thus possible only when the desert climate relents. An archaeologist usually determines on the basis of research where a specific site may be found; sometimes such sites are excavations that were begun by past explorers and then were covered over by sand or lost because of war, politics, or simple neglect. Even though archaeologists often know what they are looking for and approximately where to look, they sometimes set out to discover one thing and instead find something completely unexpected. A team of engineers may stumble over some bones or pottery shards while digging a sewage system, or local residents will come across a wall—the remnants of an ancient dwelling—as they dig foundations for new homes.

This is what happened when a sewage system was being constructed for Nazlet el-Simman, the modern village closest to the Great Pyramid of Khufu at Giza. Most of the people living there work as camel or horse drivers, as amateur guides to the Giza sites, or as vendors of postcards and souvenirs. In 1990 I appointed an Inspector to supervise the digging of the sewer so that we could follow the route of the causeway and find the Valley Temple of the Great Pyramid. But the local people were afraid that we would ruin their homes, so when I drove there one day to oversee the discovery of the Valley Temple, they tried to burn my car, an angry warning not to disrupt their village. This, of course, was not our intention at all. We did find stone blocks used by the ancient workmen to construct the causeway to the pyramid, just as I suspected we would, but we merely gathered them in the center of the village so that it would be easy for future archaeologists to locate the site.

When the people of Nazlet el-Sisi, a village at the eastern foot of the Great Pyramid, were building new houses, they found a wall consisting of layers of basalt over a limestone base. The villagers hid this fact from us and even damaged part of the wall. We were fortunate that one of them reported the discovery to us, because when I went to inspect the site, I realized that what they were about to destroy was part of the ancient man-made harbor of the Great Pyramid of Khufu, which connected with a canal to the Nile and was used to transport building stones to the Giza Plateau.

The discovery in Bahariya Oasis is only the fourth recorded instance in which an animal has made a major archaeological find in Egypt. In 1899, before he even dreamed of uncovering King Tutankhamun's tomb, the famous English archaeologist Howard Carter made one of his earlier discoveries by accident—literally. While returning to his home on the West Bank one evening, Carter's horse stumbled and fell; its hoof had struck the edge of a sealed chamber in which Carter would soon find a painted limestone statue of Mentuhotep Nebhepetre, who ruled Egypt from 2061 to 2010 B.C., the first king of the Middle Kingdom. (Carter got lucky again in 1922, when his benefactor, Lord Carnarvon, had just about given up hope of finding Tutankhamun's tomb and decided this would be the last season he would fund the dig. Carter's water boy unintentionally placed the pole of a tripod in a hole that turned out to be the first step leading down to the famous tomb, only a few feet away from where Carter's team was digging.)

In 1900, in the city of Alexandria, another Antiquities Guard drove his donkey and cart straight down into a hole in a desert road just beyond the southwestern edge of the city, near the well-known classical monument called Pompey's Pillar. He landed in a labyrinth of underground tunnels known today as Kom el-Shugafa, a complex of Alexandrian catacombs dated to the second century A.D. Like the newly discovered site at Bahariya, this is a Greco-Roman cemetery, perhaps the most famous multiple tomb in Egypt. Believed to be the burial site of a religious community, Kom el-Shugafa has thus far served as our richest source for understanding this period in ancient Egyptian history. It represents a typical fusion of Egyptian, Greek, and Roman styles of art and architecture. Mummies seem to have been buried according to religious affiliation, which serves as a good demonstration of how the three religious cultures coexisted in Egypt during the first and second centuries A.D.

The two other discoveries by animal took place on my sites, for which I can only say "il-Hamdulillah," a phrase we say every day in Egypt meaning "Thanks be to God." The first occurrence was on the Giza Plateau. I had written my dissertation on the funerary cult of the Fourth Dynasty kings Khufu, Khafre, and Menkaure, and in the course of my study, I became convinced that the tombs of the workers who had built the pyramids were located to the south of the Great Sphinx. In 1990, after returning to Egypt from the United States, I collaborated with my friend and fellow archaeologist, Mark Lehner, in searching for the tombs and the ancient work site. We mapped out a grid of ten-meter squares and opened four of them. In one we found evidence of a burial that included bones and pottery, and in another we found grain, although the digging season ended before we could interpret its significance. Then, on a very humid day in August of the same year, Mohammed Abdul Razik, former Chief of the Antiquities Guards on the Giza Plateau, came to me and said that an American woman had been riding a horse that had tripped on what appeared to be a wall. I immediately went with him to the spot, and when I saw the mud-brick wall that the horse had stumbled over and then looked directly north toward the Great Pyramid, I announced: "These are the tombs of the workers who built the pyramids!" The spot was just nine yards from where we had been digging only a few months earlier. Since 1990, statues, tombs, or skeletons have been discovered almost daily on the site. We have established the location of an upper cemetery for the artisans and a lower cemetery for the workmen who moved the stones, as well as a work site, which included an area where pottery, beer, and bread were made.

The second time providence stepped in for me in the form of an equine was, of course, at Bahariya Oasis, the now-famous site of the Valley of the Golden Mummies. A preliminary survey of the site was made by Mohammed Tiyab and Mohammed Aiady, Inspectors from the Bahariya office, immediately after the discovery, but it was not until 1999 that we decided to take a team to Bahariya to begin the excavation of the four tombs that had been surveyed, in order to establish a conservation plan to protect the site. I told my team that they should be prepared to stay at the site for at least three weeks, until it was too hot in the desert to dig anymore. Then I met with my secretary, Nashwa Gaber, who organizes every detail of my life and to whom I owe much of my success. I instructed her to call me only if anything was urgent. We packed a bus for the drive and headed out. I kept my eyes closed the whole way, thinking

**One of the first masks to emerge from the sand at the site of the Greco-Roman cemetery**

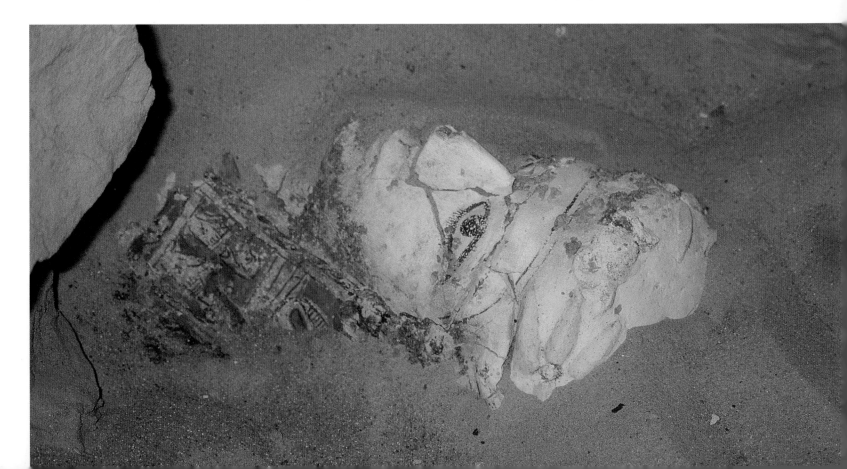

about everything I was leaving behind and trying to imagine what this site would contain.

We arrived at the local mining company's small housing community, where we had rented five apartments. The next morning after leaving at five, it took us a whole hour to drive to the site. We realized that we would have to find a place to stay in the town of El Bawiti, which is about fifteen minutes away. We settled into El Beshmo Lodge, a cottage-style hotel with an especially friendly atmosphere. We were all happier and went to a café in town to discuss our

plan for the next day's site survey. The owner of the café came to me and said, "Sir, our town is so neglected. Next time you're on TV, will you please talk about us?" Neither of us realized that I would soon be mentioning their little town in publications and programs broadcast worldwide. Bahariya has now become one of the most famous archaeological areas in the world.

When the team got to the site the next day, we walked around collecting artifacts such as pottery shards, bones, and old glass, which were littered across an area three hundred yards to the south of the Temple of Alexander the Great. From this initial survey,

El Beshmo Lodge in El Bawiti, where the excavation team and visitors stay when they are in Bahariya Oasis

*Below:* A modern mud-brick shelter on a farm near the Temple of Alexander the Great

I estimated the size of the cemetery could be nearly four square miles. The next step was to dig a sondage, a narrow trench, around the entire area to establish its boundaries. Then the architects Abdul Hamied and Hamdi mapped out a grid dividing the entire site into ten-meter squares.

Each of the six hundred squares—identical, nondescript swells of sand and rocks—was then assigned a number and an archaeologist. One square contained the tomb partially excavated by the two inspectors Aiady and Tiyab. This was Tomb 54, to which Mansour Boriak was assigned. Pickaxes and shovels began to plunge into the sand. As the sun rose higher overhead, the heat intensified, but everyone seemed too focused on their work and on what their next shovel full of sand might reveal to notice. Baskets of sand were carried away by local workers hired for the season. I noticed how weathered and bony their hands and feet were compared to those of the rest of us, who write or work in an office during the off-season. Soon the line of men passing baskets of sand from one to another grew longer as the holes dug in the desert grew deeper. The rim of some sloping shafts began to emerge, then a few stairs leading about ten feet down, then flat earth. We had reached the floor of a tomb.

It wasn't long before we struck gold. A face, a golden face beautifully molded with large obsidian eyes staring out from beneath the sand, and then an entire mummy. It was Tomb 54 that would soon prove to contain the largest number of mummies, and the best-preserved examples, of all the four squares we completed that season. It always seems that just when we sense something important is about to happen and everyone's work speeds up and excitement rises, the sun sets and we are forced to stop. We must be patient until the next day, when the light will enable us to continue. We always seem to end the day satisfied at how much has been done yet suffering from almost unbearable anticipation.

*Opposite top:* Workmen clear sand from Tomb 54, which contained the largest number of gilded mummies found to date.

*Opposite bottom:* An ancient water well in the Valley of the Golden Mummies

*Below:* The gilded mask and cartonnage chest plate of a male mummy painted with funerary scenes showing gods that will protect the deceased in the afterlife

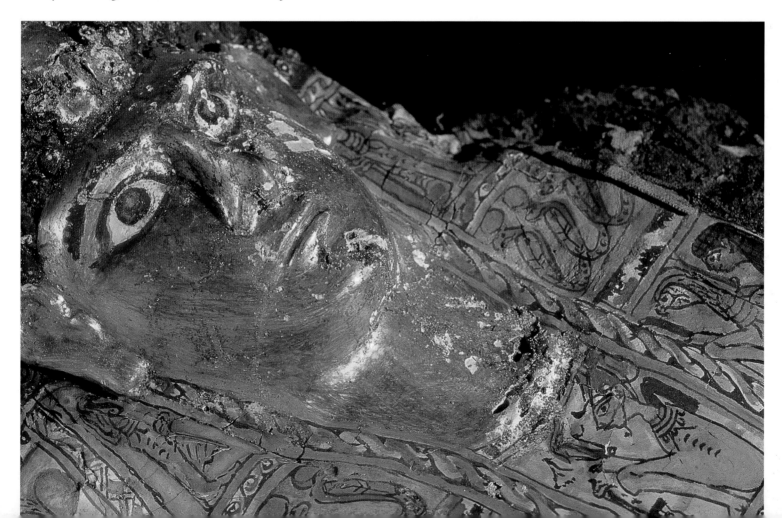

# A DAY AT THE DIG

**W**E GOT UP AT 5:00 A.M. EVERY DAY FOR THREE WEEKS, BREAKFASTED together in the lodge's restaurant, and left for the site by at least 6 o'clock so that we could begin to dig by 7:00. Although it was cold in the morning when we first gathered, the desert heated up very quickly, so we always wore several layers of clothing. The workers created a pleasant atmosphere throughout the day by singing, chanting a new verse with each bucket of sand they carried out of the tombs. I usually gave everyone half an hour at midday for tea and a snack. Otherwise, the atmosphere was intense, and my team took no other breaks during the day. The digging and brushing never stopped.

There is nothing comparable to the smell one encounters upon approaching a mummified body that has been buried for two thousand years. It is indescribable. I have become inured to the stench over the years, and my younger colleagues seem to marvel at how I can continue the work unfazed. At about the same time that Tomb 54 was producing its variously decorated mummies, Tarek el-Awady, my right-hand assistant at the office, was troweling out an area of blackened sand in Tomb 1. This black sand—caused by resin and minerals in the deteriorating organic material—is the first indication that one is getting close to a mummy. The knowledge that something mysterious is right under your hands compels you to continue working, but the closer you get to your goal, the more you want to run away. The faster you want to dig, the more carefully you have to work. Then comes the moment when you first see the gold. It is an unbelievable thrill, yet that is the moment when the stench is almost overwhelming.

As Tarek exchanged his pickax for a brush to begin uncovering his first mummy, he looked as if he were going to pass out. He is a very serious young man and a focused student, and I believe he will be one of the most influential archaeologists of his generation. I had to laugh, remembering my own early days struggling with these conflicting feelings. Pieces of the mummy's outer casing had flaked off into the sand like ashes or charcoal, but Tarek patiently brushed away the sand from around the body, until he could see that it was wrapped entirely in linen. Everyone came over to see the incredibly intricate geometric pattern in which the material had been wound around the body, each layer forming the edge of another square. Tarek appeared both proud of his first major discovery and immensely relieved when he could finally walk away from it.

Meanwhile, Mansour Boriak had been clearing Tomb 54. I first brought Mansour to work with me on the Tombs of the Pyramid Builders at Giza, and I depend on him now for all my important excavations. One must be a good administrator in order to be a good archaeologist, and Mansour is both. The northwest entrance of Tomb 54 is at the top of eight steps that lead down at a 45-degree angle to a small room and two connecting burial chambers. The first room, only about four by eight feet, is the "delivery room," where the relatives handed over the body of

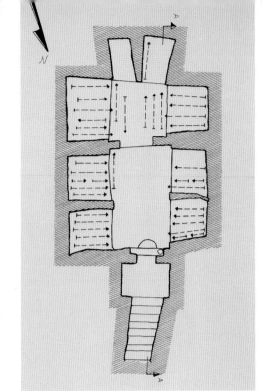

Workmen clearing Tomb 54, one of the largest discovered in the Valley of the Golden Mummies during the 1999 excavation season

*Above right:* Plan of Tomb 54

*Page 32:* Tomb 54 was so full that several mummies had been laid on the floor.

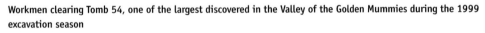

*Right:* Beyond the Antiquities Department tent, workmen begin the day at Tomb 1, the oldest tomb at the site.

*Below:* After the discovery, the guard Abdul Maugoud was reassigned to the tombsite. His donkey always liked to stand near the tombs as we worked. We began work very early in the day to avoid the intense heat of the desert.

Archaeologist Mansour Boriak brushes and blows sand away from crevices in the cartonnage and linen wrappings of one of the mummies.

*Top:* A conservator takes great care not to damage the fragile outer casings of a golden mummy in Tomb 54, while another worker continues to remove sand from a nearby niche.

*Right:* Different styles of mummies are represented in Tomb 54 with varying degrees of gold, cartonnage, and linen.

*Opposite:* The author (foreground) clears a gilded chest plate as workmen collect pieces of a stucco mask from the tomb floor.

the deceased during a funeral. The room is just big enough to enable four people to pass the mummy into the burial chamber, where four more people would receive it and lay it in its resting place. Sockets in the floor indicate there was probably a wooden door between the two rooms. The ceiling of the delivery room, which was about eight feet high, caved in long ago.

Each of the two burial chambers has four niches cut into the sandstone walls, two on each wall, which form mastabas, or benchlike platforms. The second burial chamber was especially

Tomb 54 was filled with mummies, representing different generations of the same family interred together. Two child mummies were placed between two adults, presumably their parents.

*Right:* When a married couple is buried side by side, the woman's mask is often turned toward the man's, indicating that he died before she did.

challenging to work in because of the large number of mummies within its limited space, so that only a few workmen could carry out the sand as we proceeded with the delicate work of brushing the sand from around the bodies. A total of forty-three mummies were (and still are, except for the five now in the Bahariya Museum) lined up together in every available space, some even stacked on top of each other. We concluded that this tomb must have been used by one family over several generations, since so many mummies were interred together.

The archaeologists used rocks to prop up the heads of mummies that were too tall for their niches so that they would not be damaged during the excavation.

The author brushes sand from some of the mummies in Tomb 54.

Lower-class mummies wrapped only in linen

*Left:* Visible at the bottom of the shaft of Tomb 55 are the entrances to four burial chambers, which are carved in the style of Greek temples.

*Opposite:* The lower half of each mummy is carefully wrapped in linen to form geometric patterns, a technique popularized in the Greco-Roman Period.

The structure of Tomb 55, which lies just west of Tomb 54, is very different, more like a vertical shaft. The mummies here may have been related to those buried in Tomb 54, since the tombs are close together. Instead of a set of stairs, a square shaft led us straight down to a depth of more than ten feet, where we found four burial chambers, one on each side of the shaft. The entrances to each chamber were cut into the sandstone in the style of ancient Egyptian temple entrances, with pylons on either side and a cornice over the top. The builders of this tomb obviously completed all four of the impressive entryways before beginning to dig their burial chambers, because those on the south and east were never finished or used.

The western burial chamber was closed with a large piece of sandstone, which relatives of the deceased had to move each time they wanted to bury another member of the family and which took us a few days to remove. Inside the chamber were four mummies in poor condition and some

Located in a niche of its own in Tomb 55, a mummy entirely wrapped in linen has been well preserved by the dry sand for about 2,000 years.

pottery vessels that would have contained offerings left to the gods and food for the deceased in the afterlife. Also found was a terra-cotta statue resembling Bes, the god of pleasure.

The northern burial chamber contained three skeletons, two pottery vessels, a copper anklet, and a necklace made of faience beads, in the center of which was a *wedjat*-eye amulet. This eye of the falcon-god Horus was believed to keep evil spirits at bay and to assist in the deceased's journey through the underworld. The individuals buried here may have been of a lower class, since they seem to have been wrapped in linen in a relatively careless manner.

Despite the fact that two of the chambers had not been used, we found another mummy that had been stashed alone at the bottom of the shaft, beautifully wrapped in classic New Kingdom fashion and surprisingly well preserved. Since this mummy did not appear to have any close relatives and was particularly photogenic, I would later call it "Mr. or Mrs. X" and select it to go to Cairo for X-ray studies as a representative of the Valley of the Golden Mummies (see chapter 5).

The next tomb we found, Tomb 62, turned out to be the largest in size and contained a total of thirty-two mummies. Mahmoud Afifi, Chief Antiquities Inspector of the Pyramids, was in charge of this tomb. He is very soft-spoken in my presence but reveals quite another personality with the others. He always stayed up later than everyone else, smoking a *shisha* pipe in the courtyard, a water pipe commonly used by Egyptians for smoking tobacco. Tomb 62 was cut into the rock on two axes, one extending to the southwest and the other to the southeast. The entrance is

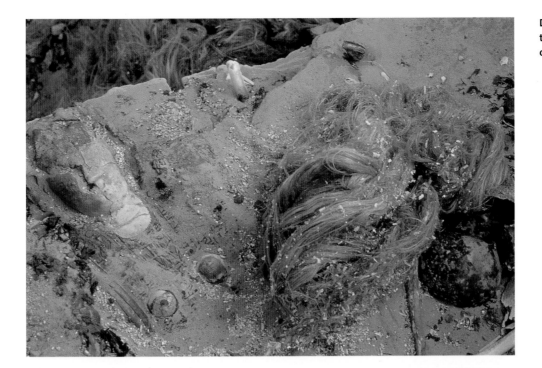

Dried material collected by local farmers from date trees cover the mummies to protect their fragile condition.

The breasts of women mummies were molded from cartonnage and sometimes gilded during the Greco-Roman Period.

**Excavation work begins on Tomb 62.**

down a narrow stairway that went about ten feet down to a delivery room, which leads into two burial chambers. The first contains four short shafts cut into the walls and the second has three; a third chamber was apparently attempted but abandoned. The mummies were found lying in many different directions, unlike those of earlier periods whose heads always faced east. Some were buried inside wooden coffins, one of them a child, while others were covered with cartonnage, a type of plaster mixed with linen to form a hard shell on the chest and head of the mummy. Most of the bodies, however, had been mummified by being simply wrapped in linen, so they were partially crushed when the ceiling collapsed on them at some point in the past. Some of the mummies had been left on the floor rather than in the niches because the tomb was too full, and a few of the heads had come off.

Within shaft A of the first burial chamber, alongside the mummies, coins were found inscribed with several intriguing figures that can be dated to the Ptolemaic Period (305–30 B.C.). One of the coins is carved with a portrait of Cleopatra VII, the last of the Greek rulers, which made me realize that we would need a Greco-Roman scholar to decipher many of the objects we were finding. We also found two unique pottery vessels, which I will describe in more detail in chapter 4.

Tomb 64 was the last to be excavated that season, and the only one with its ceiling intact. Eleven steps lead from north to south into a small delivery room, where a hole in the floor forms the entrance into the burial chamber. We set up a ladder to get down into the hole (wondering if

saw three niches cut into the walls. It seems that after
another two shafts were cut into the stone to the left
le we found a child wrapped in linen, and on the right
condition. Next to them lay the mummy of a child
details of his face had been painted over a thin layer
wooden model and then placed on the mummy after
ly on the mummy itself, as with some of the other
ighteen mummies.

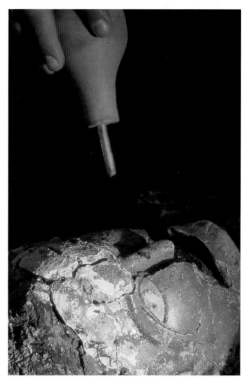

Squeezing air from a blower is one of the best techniques an archaeologist has for the delicate process of clearing sand from a mummy.

*Left:* A gilded mask found cracked and crumbling

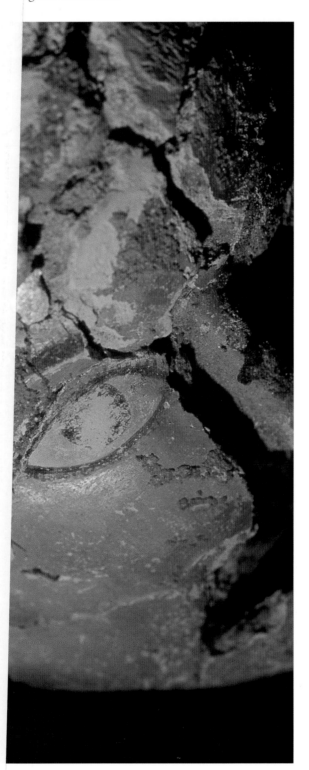

A workman cleans the clay coffins found in Tomb 1

*Below:* A guard checks on Tomb 1 while the workmen are on a tea break.

*Opposite top:* Tomb 1 is the only tomb with wall paintings. Two images of the jackal-god Anubis as lord of the cemetery appear at the entrance to the burial chamber, to protect the deceased on the journey through the underworld.

*Opposite bottom:* Pictures of Anubis painted directly on the sandstone entrance to the burial chamber of Tomb 1

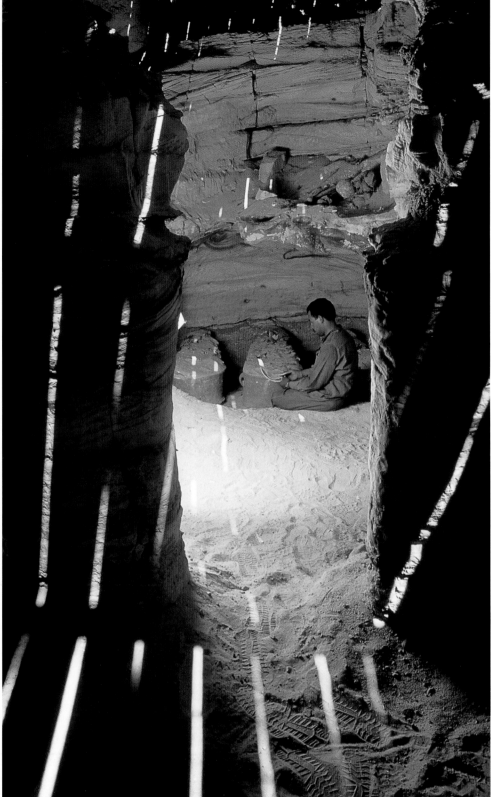

Tomb 1 was quite large but contained only four mummies. I believe that this is an older tomb, because the few mummies buried there suggest that there was still plenty of space in the cemetery and because a mummy found in the top shaft of the burial chamber was buried in a coffin with an anthropoid, or human-shaped, lid, indicating an earlier style of mummification. Also, this is the only tomb we have yet found that has an inscription with two colored drawings of Anubis, the god of embalming, guarding the burial-chamber entrance (see chapter 8). The architecture of the tomb also differed slightly from the others at the site, in that there was a separate room between the delivery room and the burial chamber. This may have been where relatives paid later

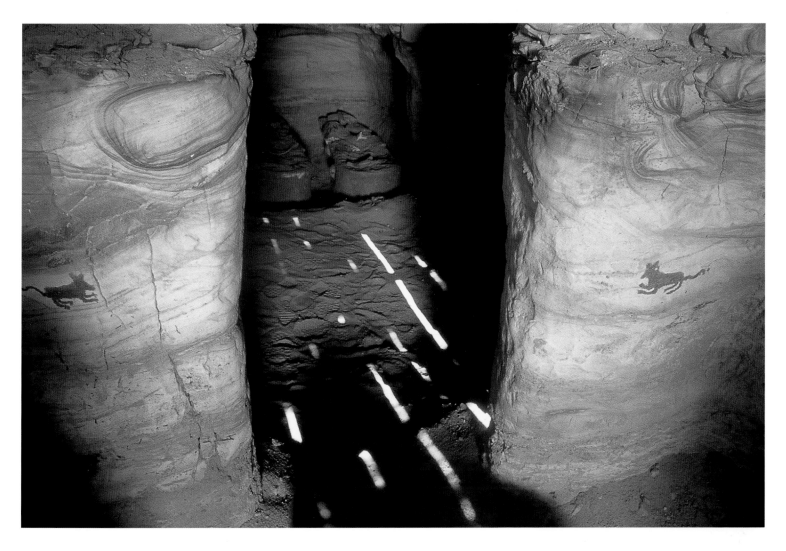

visits to the deceased to make offerings, or it may have been a storage room, both uses reflecting ancient Egyptian practice. Several styles of pottery cups and vessels littered the floor of this "relative room." The burial chamber is split into two sections with niches cut one on top of the other in the Roman style.

As we ended the excavation for the season, we took three hours to survey the rest of the site in order to plan our excavation for the next season. North of Tomb I, Tarek found an unexcavated tomb in which there was a cylindrical anthropoid coffin containing a mummy in poor condition, wrapped in linen. The top of the coffin is made of fired clay and is in excellent condition. There are six handles, two on the lid, and four on the body of the coffin. The face of a man and his headdress are painted on the lid in yellow, black, and reddish brown; the face is broad and flat, the forehead narrow, the eyebrows long. The nose and eyebrows, which blend into a single line, are the only raised features modeled on the face. The headdress, which is ancient Egyptian in style, extends down the sides of the face with dark and light horizontal lines, suggesting a pharaoh's headdress. The collar, made of four rows of curving lines, is a stylized version of the *wskh*, a type of collar with religious and ritual significance associated with the creator god Atum.

Unlike older Egyptian tombs, none of the rooms, steps, or shafts found in the Valley of the Golden Mummies was cut with exact angles, and none of the walls bears any inscriptions,

The molded face of the anthropoid coffin is painted with yellow, black, and red colors.

*Left:* A conservator cleans the outside of the cylindrical anthropoid coffin at the entrance of the tomb.

*Opposite:* The only anthropoid coffin found in the Greco-Roman cemetery to date contains a linen-wrapped mummy. A separate piece, molded to look like the head of the mummy, fits on top of the clay coffin.

paintings, or relief carvings, with the exception of the Anubis pictures in Tomb I. It is therefore impossible to determine exactly who these mummies once were. The decorative style of the mummies and the tomb structures are uniquely Greco-Roman, however, and we have concluded that the cemetery continued to be used from about 332 B.C., during the reign of Alexander the Great, throughout the period of Roman rule, when life in the Oasis reached its peak, and perhaps even beyond that, into the fourth or fifth century A.D.

Gilded mummies representing the wealthier population of Bahariya Oasis, possibly merchants and land owners, during the Greco-Roman Period

*Right:* Some of the most lavishly decorated mummies found in the cemetery to date

We were always exhausted by the time we returned to the hotel with the setting sun. Since we were dirty, hungry, and tired, it was difficult to choose which we needed most—a shower, dinner, or bed. My first order of business after washing up was always to relax in the courtyard with a *shisha* pipe, which Sobhy, a member of the hotel staff, prepared for me each evening. At 8 P.M. we shared dinner at the hotel restaurant with the National Geographic crew. Before going to my room, I made sure to tell everyone that if they got to the vans even one minute late the next morning, they could take the next bus back to Cairo. Almost everyone would be asleep by 9:30. The evenings were lively, however, as Mansour would tell jokes and do imitations of everyone for the members of the team sitting in the courtyard. Every night a few of the villagers would come around to hear what we were finding at the site, and we could pass around the shisha pipe and tell stories of our day. One night, the mayor of the town came and told the stories of how Bahariya had changed since 1949, when the late Egyptian archaeologist Ahmed Fakhry had last visited the Oasis to explore and describe its unusual monuments.

After covering the mummies for the night, a guard locks up Tomb 54, which is now covered with a wooden roof to replace the original sandstone ceiling, which had collapsed.

# THE GOLDEN MUMMIES

FOUR DISTINCT MUMMY TYPES WERE DISCOVERED IN THE FIRST FIVE TOMBS THAT we excavated. The first type, mummies encased with cartonnage and gold, represents wealthy individuals, possibly local merchants. About sixty of these mummies were found with golden masks, and some of them have gold chest plates covering their chests embossed with modeled images of Egyptian gods. Mummies A and B, described below, are of this type. I remember one morning during the excavation when their gilded faces looked especially impressive. The team's energy always seemed to wear down under the increasing heat as the sun rose higher, but because the tombs were below the surface of the sand, we did not feel the full force of the sun until it was almost directly overhead. Then we usually took our short noon break. On this day the sun's rays suddenly shone into our working area and glanced off some of the golden mummies. The light was almost blinding, and my heart pounded with excitement. It amazed us all each time we uncovered another gilded mummy and realized that this was the largest undisturbed burial site ever found representing such amassed wealth.

The second type of mummy is wrapped in linen, and parts of the upper body are encased in cartonnage that covers the chest area and is usually painted with depictions of funerary deities. Our otherwise imperturbable archaeologists were startled on several occasions while uncovering this particular type of mummy because many of them have very lifelike eyes. As you slowly brush sand away from around a mummy, you never quite know the exact moment when the mummy's features will emerge. Suddenly its eyes will pop out from the sand, staring directly at you. These eyes are beautifully crafted and inlaid with white marble around a black obsidian iris. Some of the eyes look as if they have just been polished, and at midday they reflect light in a way that gives them a kind of glint. In some cases, the eyes are even set in bronze or copper with thin spikes for eyelashes, which makes the effect even more uncannily realistic. In a few of the mummies the eyes had somehow shifted so that they pointed in different directions, and the effect that they made, looking every which way out of the sand as we worked, was quite unnerving.

The third type of mummy is wrapped only in linen, often in geometric patterns, with no painting or gilding. These mummies represent members of the middle class, possibly farm owners. The fourth type of mummy is carelessly wrapped, and in several cases the linen has unraveled and the bodies have almost completely carbonized. These were undoubtedly the mummies of poorer individuals in the community.

Of all the 105 mummies uncovered in the Valley of the Golden Mummies, six are now on view at the Bahariya Museum. Before we moved them, Nasry Iskander, Chief Conservator for the Royal Mummies at the Egyptian Museum in Cairo, had to prepare our mummies to be lifted from their niches. Nasry is well known to anyone who has ever filmed a documentary or made

This gilded couple must have enjoyed considerable wealth during their lifetime to be able to afford such an expensive type of mummification. Couples were buried next to each other so that they could be together in the afterlife.

*Right:* The damaged mask of a mummy whose inner linen wrapping was blackened, perhaps with resin.

*Below:* One of several mummies found at the site with inlaid eyes of white marble and black obsidian surrounded by a copper fringe made to look like eyelashes. Parts of the gilded stucco have chipped off to reveal the layers of linen beneath.

*Page 52:* Stucco masks of the Greco-Roman Period were molded to give the mummy's outer casing a realistic appearance, perhaps so that the *ba* of the deceased could recognize the body and rejoin it in the afterlife.

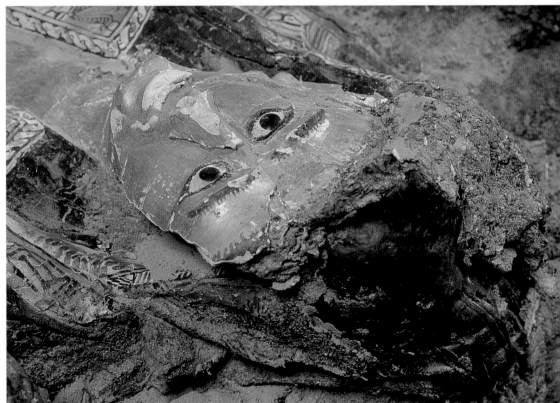

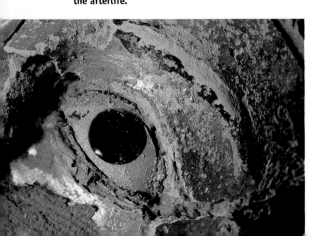

Linen dyed in various colors has been wrapped around this mummy's feet in typically Roman fashion to form diamond-shaped patterns.

*Top:* Two child mummies lie between adults, presumably their parents. In Greco-Roman times, people were buried in mass graves in family groups.

*Left:* A conservator wears protective gloves as he brushes a freshly uncovered mummy in Tomb 54.

a study of the royal mummies. He cleans each mummy we find with great care and applies chemicals to their outer casings, which always stirs up decaying organic particles and necessitates his wearing a mask as he works. The golden mummies that were selected to go to the museum in Bahariya were those that were in the best condition and would be better off being preserved in a museum setting.

MUMMY A  This was found next to Mummy B in Tomb 54 and represents the first mummy type. He is completely wrapped in linen with a cartonnage chest plate, and his entire chest and head are covered with a brilliant layer of gold. The face is long and narrow and appears to be that of a man about fifty years old. He wears a headband inlaid with colored pieces of faience and semiprecious stones. Around the forehead are modeled leaves and flowers with a uraeus in the center. At the sides of his neck below the ears are the goddesses Isis and Nephtys protecting the deceased with their wings. During the Greco-Roman Period, it was not uncommon for royal symbols, such as the uraeus, to be used by nonroyal persons.

Mummy A, now in the Bahariya Museum, is adorned with a gilded uraeus and a headband inlaid with faience and semiprecious stones in imitation of a royal crown.

*Above left:* The gilded and inlaid chest plate of Mummy A, showing molded images of the goddess Maat stretching her wings, two of the sons of Horus, beneath her, and the god Thoth as an ibis below

*Opposite:* The mummy of a man gilded and inlaid with Egyptian motifs in Greco-Roman style (Mummy A)

Mummy A is the best preserved of the male golden mummies found to date.

*Below:* Mummy B, now in the Bahariya Museum, is the best-preserved female golden mummy.

*Opposite:* The gilded mask and chest plate of a female mummy (Mummy B)

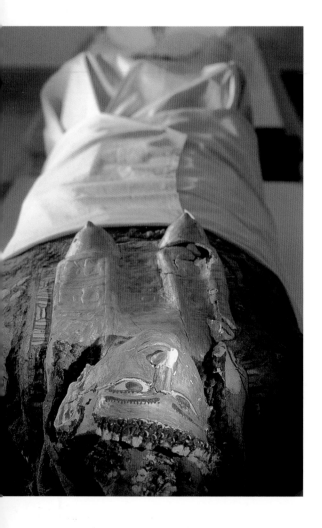

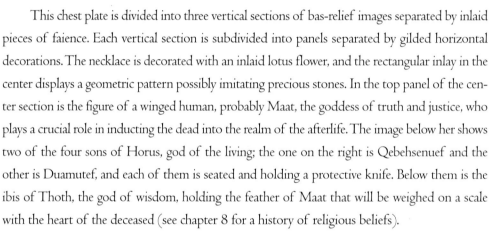

This chest plate is divided into three vertical sections of bas-relief images separated by inlaid pieces of faience. Each vertical section is subdivided into panels separated by gilded horizontal decorations. The necklace is decorated with an inlaid lotus flower, and the rectangular inlay in the center displays a geometric pattern possibly imitating precious stones. In the top panel of the center section is the figure of a winged human, probably Maat, the goddess of truth and justice, who plays a crucial role in inducting the dead into the realm of the afterlife. The image below her shows two of the four sons of Horus, god of the living; the one on the right is Qebehsenuef and the other is Duamutef, and each of them is seated and holding a protective knife. Below them is the ibis of Thoth, the god of wisdom, holding the feather of Maat that will be weighed on a scale with the heart of the deceased (see chapter 8 for a history of religious beliefs).

The figure at the top of the section at the right as one faces the mummy is one of the four sons of Horus, whose face cannot be identified. Below him is another son, Imsety, seated and holding a knife, and below him are two sons, Imsety on the right and Duamutef on the left. The bottom panel is a jackal figure representing Anubis, the god of embalming, who holds the symbol of rebirth and regeneration.

The section at the left shows, from the top: Qebehsenuef seated with a knife; Imsety also seated with a knife; and below him the two standing figures of Qebehsenuef and Hapy together. At the bottom, Anubis is shown in a mirror image of the depiction on the right side.

MUMMY B   This gilded mummy of a woman from Tomb 54 really caught my eye when we first began our excavation, and her image stayed with me for many weeks after we closed down the excavation for the season. She was found next to Mummy A, who I believe is her husband. They are gilded and decorated in exactly the same way and were fitted closely together in a narrow niche of their own. What is most striking about this couple is that her head is slightly tilted to her right, so that she seems to be gazing lovingly upon her spouse throughout eternity. He must

A thin layer of gold was painted on the cartonnage mask and chest plate after they were molded into realistic features around the elaborate linen wrapping.

*Top:* This mummy appears to be smiling, a rare sight.

This painted image between the gilded breasts of Mummy B shows a bull, probably the god Serapis, whose main cult was at Alexandria during the Greco-Roman Period.

*Top:* Articulated breasts were typically found on female mummies of the Greco-Roman Period.

have died before she did, and she may have asked to be placed next to him. Another unique feature of Mummy B is her Mona Lisa-like smile, which lends a touching quality to her face, as if she were pleased to be with her husband. Smiling mummies are very rare. Perhaps she was known in life for her pleasant countenance and perpetual laughter. One cannot help but imagine what the personalities of the mummies were like as one looks at the distinctive, expressive way in which they were depicted. A feature commonly found in females mummified in the Greco-Roman style is the articulation of breasts and nipples to distinguish their feminine nature. The breasts of Mummy B are rather low on the chest and gilded like the rest of her chest and face.

As on the other mummies, the chest plate is divided into three sections. Below her neck in the central section is a coffin from which emerge a head and two wings, perhaps signifying the figure of Isis protecting the coffin of the deceased. Anubis is depicted below, and in the bottom section are three painted squares, one black, the second light red, and the third containing a black bull, probably Serapis, the sacred bull, with a sun disk between its horns. The section to the right has at the top three cobras bearing sun disks, and the two panels below each show two of the sons of Horus; these scenes are mirrored on the left side but with the other two sons. On the side of the neck, below the ears, are the figures of Isis and Nephtys protecting the deceased with their wings. Painted cartonnage is used to form the curly black hair of the mummy's mask and the decorative rows that surround the pictorial scenes.

MUMMY C  This mummy, which is of the second type, was also found in Tomb 54. It was first wrapped in several layers of linen, and then the chest, shoulders, neck, and head were completely covered with a thick layer of cartonnage painted with traditional images of funerary deities, which in earlier times were usually inscribed on burial-chamber walls. The mask of the deceased was carefully modeled in stucco to look like that of a young man and then it was covered with a

*Below:* This view of the top of the crown on Mummy C shows the gold relief of a stylized falcon representing Horus topped with a sun disk and two cobras.

*Below left:* Mummy C, now in the Bahariya Museum, displays all the three layers of mummification—the geometrically overlapping layers of linen, the painted cartonnage modeled on top of the upper body and around its head and then the gilding over the face.

**The uraeus on the forehead was reserved in ancient Egypt for royalty, but it was adopted by nonroyal individuals during the Greco-Roman Period.**

thin layer of gold. A circular crown made of stucco was molded to resemble four rows of leaves and flowers, a typically Greek motif based on a hero's wreath. In the center of the crown is a cobra, the protective uraeus, a royal symbol that indicates the high status of this individual in the community. On the flat top of the crown is a gilded, molded image of a falcon in flight, with two feathers extending from each wing similar to those of Maat. On the head of the falcon is a sun disk from which emerge two protective cobras. The falcon represents Horus but is stylized in a unique blend of Egyptian and Greek imagery.

The mummy's chest plate is divided by black painted lines into the three vertical sections, each filled with images of gods that can protect him and assist in his journey through the under-

Funerary scenes painted on the cartonnage of Mummy C show Osiris, king of the underworld, seated before an offering table with two of the four sons of Horus: Hapy with a human head and Duamutef with the head of a jackal.

*Below:* The stucco wig of Mummy C shows black curls in the Greek style. Images of gods traditionally depicted on the walls of burial chambers were painted directly on the mummy in the Greco-Roman Period.

world. On the upper panel of the center section, Osiris, ruler of the underworld, is shown wearing a crown and seated before an offering table. He holds two different types of royal scepters in his hand. Below Osiris is an ibis representing the god Thoth, seated on a hieroglyphic sign meaning "lord." The feather of Maat extends from the ibis's leg, and at the bottom are decorative triangular shapes.

Above the top of the section on the right is a fragmentary standing figure that may be the god Horus, who holds an unidentified object in his hand. Below him are three cobras in a row with sun disks on their heads, included to afford protection to the deceased. The scene below the cobras shows two seated sons of Horus, Qebehsenuef on the left and Imsety on the right, each holding knives. Below them a standing figure of the deceased wearing a headdress offering an object that may represent an incense burner to the figures of Osiris and Thoth in the center.

The images on the left nearly mirror those on the opposite side. The figure at the top, also fragmentary, may represent Seth, the god of evil. The sections below depict the three cobras and below them the two other sons of Horus, Duamutef on the left and Hapy on the right. The bottom panel shows the deceased holding a stand on which is pictured the jackal-god Wepwawet, who will open the gates to the underworld, as well as crossed scepters like those held by Osiris.

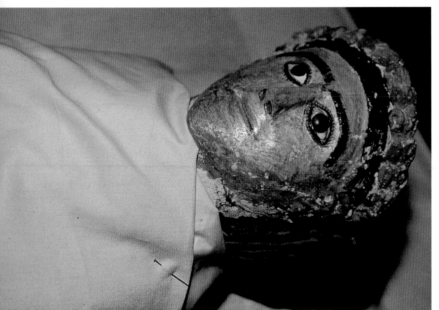

THE BOY MUMMY  This little body, only thirty-three-and-a-half inches long, belongs to that of a boy we think was about five years old. His entire body is wrapped in linen, and his head is covered with a gilded mask made of stucco. His eyes, thick eyebrows, and short hair are painted black, and his small headband is colored red and yellow to look like flowers and leaves. His nose and lips are very narrow. The mummy was found in Tomb 54 next to a girl of the same height, and we assume that they were brother and sister; they are both classified as the third type of mummy we found.

THE GIRL MUMMY  This small female mummy is wrapped expertly in the same geo-metric pattern as the boy mummy, with a similar mask of stucco, whose defined eyes and eye-brows are somewhat more feminine. Like Mummy B, she displays a slight smile. Both of her ears have survived, although the boy mummy's left ear has fallen off. Her hair is shown curly and short in a kind of circle colored white and black. Her mask is extended to her chest, where scenes of the four sons of Horus appear; at each side are the cobras and images of Anubis.

The girl mummy from Tomb 54, now in the Bahariya Museum. A few of her black curls, which were molded in stucco and then painted, have fallen off.

*Top:* Uncovering the painted cartonnage of the girl mummy

*Left:* The gilded girl mummy smiles from her resting place.

The mummy of a young woman painted to look like a bride for her marriage in the afterlife

THE BRIDE MUMMY   One of the mummies, who remains in Tomb 54, was a young female whose stucco mask was painted to resemble that of a bride. Her eyes and eyebrows are dark, and her face is white with red circles on her cheeks indicating makeup. On her head is a headdress, and a necklace is painted on her chest plate. Beneath the chest plate, painted on the cartonnage, are images of the four sons of Horus, the cobras with sun disks, and an ibis. The mummy's breasts, also modeled from cartonnage, are smaller than those of the older female mummies and are painted a rose color.

I believe that this young woman must have died shortly before her marriage, so that the family prepared her body as if she were a bride. An ancient Egyptian belief held that if one did not get married in one's lifetime, the wedding would take place in the afterlife. I found the happy,

These stucco masks (now in the Bahariya Museum), found separated from their respective mummies, reveal the Greek style in the way the hair, headbands, and collars are molded and painted.

innocent-looking countenance of this mummy very touching. I could just imagine her preparing for her wedding day and her family and fiancé mourning her early death.

The scenes that appear on the cartonnage chest plates are abbreviated forms of the vignettes that accompanied funerary texts containing spells, which were used to insure the deceased's entrance into the underworld. These texts were carved in bas-relief, which was often painted, on tomb walls during the Old Kingdom, but by the Middle Kingdom they appeared on coffins (as *Coffin Texts*), and eventually, by the New Kingdom, they appeared on inscribed papyri, known by the collective title *The Book of the Dead,* which were buried along with the deceased. By the time the deceased were entombed in the Valley of the Golden Mummies, these images were painted directly on the

The site at sunset after the excavation team has returned to the hotel

bodies of the mummies. The most important figures are those of Osiris, god of the dead, who presides over the judgment of the deceased; his son, Horus, the falcon-god of the sun and ruler of the living; the jackal-headed Anubis, also the god of embalming and keeper of the keys to the underworld; Thoth, god of wisdom; and Maat, goddess of truth and justice, whose feather is weighed against the deceased's heart to test its purity as Osiris decides whether or not to grant eternal life. (Chapter 8 contains a more detailed description of Egyptian religious beliefs.)

In ancient Egypt, the uraeus, or cobra, usually appeared only on the pharaoh's crown, but in the Roman Period, elements such as crowns, scenes of the unification of Upper and Lower Egypt, the use of the king-god's beard, and the uraeus, once reserved only for the royal cult, were used by the general populace. The gods depicted on the chest plates are purely Egyptian, although some are rendered in the Roman style, specifically in their hairstyles, headdresses, and realistic features, and in their stylized depictions, especially Horus on Mummy C. This suggests that the population still adhered to traditional Egyptian beliefs in spite of their adoption of Roman artistic style. The way in which the mummy masks were made and how they were attached to the mummies can, like style and imagery, also be used as criteria for dating. In the case of the golden mummies that we have found so far, the hairstyle, the headdress, and the articulation of breasts suggest that these mummies date to the end of the first century A.D., but some may prove to be even older based on

the date of the artifacts found in the tombs. The exact time period during which the cemetery was used cannot be fully determined until after we complete the excavation, which will not be for several decades.

In the meantime, a picture of the residents of Bahariya Oasis during the Greco-Roman Period is emerging through the excavation of the golden mummies, the artifacts found in their tombs, the scenes depicted on their chest plates, other monuments found in Bahariya, and even the study of the residents today. Although no remains of Roman rulers have yet been found, we know that they would have had the most elaborate burial styles. We assume that most of the golden mummies represent the second level, a wealthy and relatively high-ranking class of merchants and landowners just below that of the rulers.

**A guard checks the site after everyone has left at the end of the day.**

# ARTIFACTS
# FROM THE TOMBS

**M**ANY WONDERFUL ARTIFACTS WERE FOUND INSIDE THE TOMBS IN THE Valley of the Golden Mummies, often placed alongside mummies as offerings to the gods or for use in the afterlife. Funerary objects can provide archaeologists with a good idea of the religious and economic status of the people buried with them, and the presence of statuettes reveal the extent to which certain gods and goddesses were worshiped. For example, a wooden head of Sekhmet, the lioness-goddess of war, was placed at the feet of three mummies as a measure of protection. Fifteen and a half inches in height, the head is carved in great detail; its black-painted open mouth and dark inlaid eyes indicate the goddess's power.

This object reminded me of our epigrapher, Noha Abdul Hafiz, the only female member of our team. She has the broad face of a pharaonic Egyptian woman and exceptionally patient hands, which can do the delicate work required to draw each new discovery. At Bahariya she usually worked very quietly, but if she was angry, she became like the lioness. She would move from tomb to tomb as the mummies were discovered, spreading tracing paper over their chests to copy their scenes. Every day she drew all of the uncovered artifacts inside the nearby antiquities tent, including the detailed coins and jewelry. It was a challenging job to keep up with the rate of discovery, and I was always very hard on her. I must say that I think she worked the hardest of all of us.

Several clay statuettes of motherhood goddesses buried with the dead indicate that the ancient concept of rebirth continued through the Greco-Roman period. This type of stylized female body, modeled with large hips and breasts, was an important image as early as the Predynastic Period, not just in Egypt but also in Greece and elsewhere in the Mediterranean. It is not surprising, therefore, that these figures would still be used at this time, when the great mother figure, Isis, was often pictured nursing her son Horus to make him strong enough to avenge the death of his father, Osiris. Every living king was the representative of Horus, the sun-god, and women were considered the pillars of civilization. In spite of the traditional nature of these images, however, Mansour Boriak noted in his log that the artistic style of these particular figures are unique to Bahariya Oasis in the way their breasts, faces, and bases were modeled.

For example, the lower half of one seven-inch-high statuette appears to be a cylinder rather than a modeled body with legs. The figure has thick lips and eyebrows, large ears, short hair, and large breasts, between which is painted a dark line. Another, slightly larger figure has both male and female features, with a rectangular head, brown hair, large nose, thick lips, and a short neck. Its breasts are large, indicating fertility; a strange feature is that one hand rests beneath a breast, perhaps as a symbol of life-giving regeneration.

Women were also commonly depicted as mourners in Egyptian art. In New Kingdom tombs

*Above and right:* Motherhood statuettes made of clay were symbols of fertility.

*Page 70:* A collection of jewelry, including a clay amulet representing fertility. Amulets like this were strung with beads on necklaces intended for ritualistic use.

weeping figures were painted on walls, but in this Greco-Roman cemetery they appear as statuettes. It was part of the ancient funerary ritual to hire professional mourners to follow the dead to their graves, and this tradition still exists in some villages in Upper Egypt, where local women are paid to wear black dresses and walk behind the funeral procession waving their hands and striking themselves in grief. We assume that the purpose of these statuettes was to weep for the deceased. Two of the terra-cotta mourners have their hands over their eyes, and a

third has her hands on her head. We have so far found only four of these figures, which were buried with the wealthiest mummies in Tomb 54. Perhaps this was an honor reserved for people in high positions.

Another ancient funerary tradition involved the use of what appear to be small liquor glasses. Their function is not absolutely clear, but it is possible that they were filled with tears for the deceased and left behind in the tombs. Some archaeologists have speculated that they are water or wine glasses, or that they were filled with some kind of ointment or kohl, a substance women commonly used around their eyes. In any case, eight of these were found lying beside the mummies in Tomb 54.

Toys carved in the shapes of animals were found near the children's mummies, and were presumably to be played with in the afterlife. One special toy was a terra-cotta horse whose mane and tail were modeled in great detail; the two holes that represent the eyes may have been used to hang the toy by a string.

Two types of jewelry were found with the female mummies in a few of the tombs: items that had been worn in daily life and those that were wrapped with the mummies for use in the after-life. Recovered from one skeleton's leg was a pair of heavy copper anklets, which could be opened on one side. There were three bracelets of black glass, two of bright blue glass, and others with bright green-and-yellow bas-relief decorations. Three bracelets were made of ivory.

Rings were found scattered around the mummies whose wrappings had all but come off, each of them fashioned in the same way—a thin wire band with a flat, square piece on top. Four

**Glass vessels found around the mummies may have contained ointments or kohl for use in the afterlife, but it is also possible that they held the symbolic tears of those who mourned the deceased.**

*Top right:* **This clay horse was interred with a child mummy so that the deceased would have a toy to play with in the afterlife.**

*Top left:* **Statuettes of mourning women putting their hands over their eyes or on top of their heads will weep for the deceased throughout eternity.**

This ivory bracelet was not worn by a mummy but was found next to one for ritual use in the afterlife.

*Top:* This faience bracelet also had a ritual purpose and was not worn to adorn the deceased.

of the rings were bronze and one was silver. Another ring found on the finger of a young woman was made of black glass.

There were many necklaces. One, made of dark blue glass with black and yellow beads, had a large agate stone in the middle. A young female mummy wore a necklace made of different shapes and colored stones, including red agate. Another necklace was made of glass beads in vibrant yellow, dark blue, and black, with a blue faience bead, three chains, and such semiprecious stones as amber and onyx. At the center of one necklace was a blue faience *wedjat*-eye amulet, the eye of Horus used to ward off evil. Some of the necklaces were made of gray slate. In the dust were recovered loose beads of all kinds from broken necklaces, bracelets, and anklets.

*Left and opposite:* Different types of faience neck-laces found in tombs for use in the afterlife

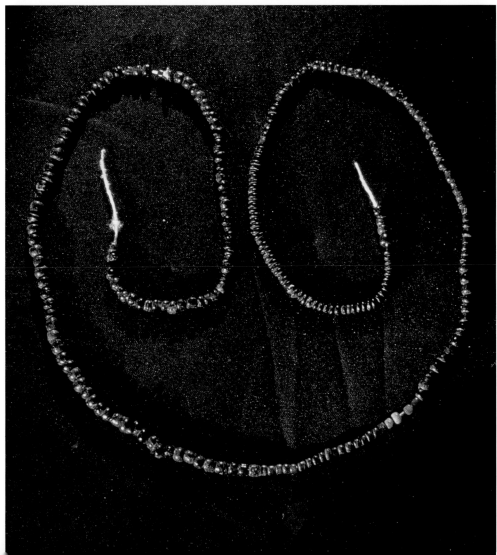

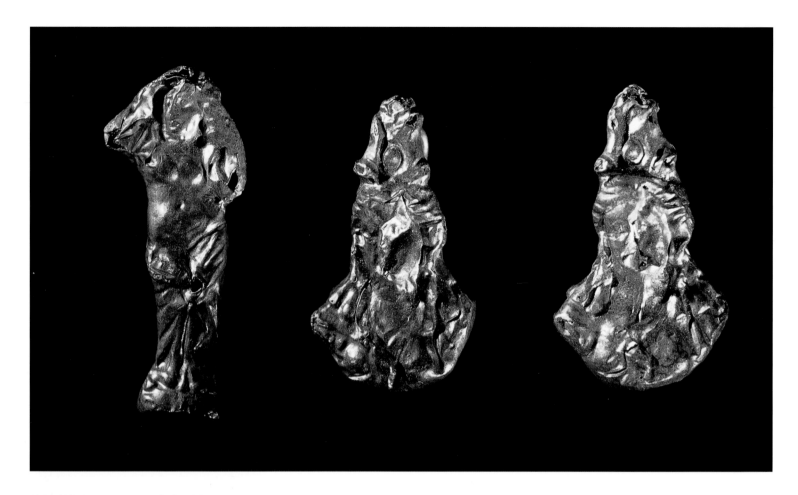

Only one thin silver hoop earring was found, along with a small vessel still containing kohl. The only gold jewelry we found was in the form of three earrings. The matching pair was decorated with the face of a god, perhaps Serapis with a sun disk on top of his head. The single earring shows a woman with breasts standing with her hands on her head, perhaps Hathor, the goddess of beauty, or her Greek equivalent, Aphrodite.

Some funerary jewelry interred for ritualistic purposes was placed on or next to the mummies and wrapped with linen. Carved miniature figurines of gods were strung together with round beads that resemble coffee beans; their purpose was to protect the deceased and help insure their resurrection. Two funerary necklaces found in Tomb 54 had a chain of motherhood goddesses and phalluses, talismans for continued regeneration. Another contained seven amulets: a horse, the jackal-god Wepwawet, a circle with a hole that perhaps represents the vagina and hence rebirth, a fertility goddess, a phallus, a green faience amulet signifying rebirth, and another phallus, which may signify the god Min, god of fertility. Other mummies had similar amulets to which had been added the figure of a bride, a star, or a falcon representing Horus.

Most of the artifacts found in the tombs were different types of unglazed pottery, much of which was left surprisingly undamaged. As with jewelry, the pottery can also be separated into two categories: those used in daily life and those intended for ritualistic purposes. The study of pottery can teach us much about the daily culture of a region. In this case, a large number of wine jars, cups, and amphoras for wine storage were interred with the mummies as offerings to the

gods, perhaps reflecting how central the wine trade was in the life of Oasis inhabitants during the Greco-Roman Period. Several jars were made in the form of the god Bes, some of them painted red like the wine they may have contained, one of them with a lid shaped like a black crown. This group of jars confirms the assumption that the god of pleasure had a special significance for the people of the Oasis.

Another type of artifact includes four ceramic dough vats of various traditional shapes and sizes. Dough vats have also been discovered in the Fifth Dynasty tomb of Ti at Saqqara and at the bakery in Mark Lehner's site east of the Tombs of the Pyramid Builders on the Giza Plateau. Other pieces of pottery include cylindrical oil and grain storage vessels with handles, water flasks, cooking pots, food bowls, and offering dishes, one of them shaped like a flower. The water vessels are similar to those used for water storage in Egyptian villages today. The oil jars with narrow spouts and the lamps were all used in daily life.

Funerary pottery imitates the pottery of daily life, but it is generally smaller in scale and

A water vessel nearly five inches high

*Above left:* This pottery wine jar with two handles is only about four inches high.

*Opposite top:* Roman-style gold earrings found in Tomb 54; the one on the left is made in the form of a goddess. These earrings had symbolic significance and were not made to be worn.

*Opposite bottom:* This three-inch-high pottery vessel, decorated with a lotus flower, may have been used to hold cosmetics, such as ointment or perfume, for use in the afterlife.

**Bronze coins from the Greco-Roman Period**

*Below:* Coin found in Tomb 55 portraying Cleopatra VII, last of the Ptolemaic rulers

*Below right:* Line drawing of the different coins found in tombs in the Valley of the Golden Mummies

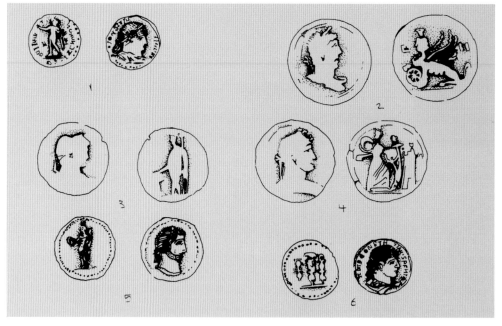

*Opposite top:* A collection of artifacts, including a painted mummy mask, a pottery vessel with the face of Bes, water vessels, coins, and a painted wooden panel showing the figure of Osiris as a wooden statue being crowned by Horus and Anubis.

*Opposite bottom:* One side of the wooden panel found in a tomb in the Valley of the Golden Mummies, showing painted scenes

located in a different part of the tomb, near the heads and legs of the mummies, presumably for use in the afterlife. Small wine cups were often left near the mummies so that the deceased could enjoy the same activities throughout eternity that they did in life.

Most of the twenty Greek and Roman bronze coins we found were wrapped in the hands of mummies, perhaps to be used to bribe the ferryman who would transport them in the solar boat to the underworld. The coins have intriguing figures on both sides; these have not yet been studied but we believe them to represent emperors or gods. One portrait is clearly that of

Cleopatra VII, who ruled from 51 to 30 B.C., until the Roman usurped her leadership. Salah Ahmed Ali, a native of Bahariya who graduated from the Conservation Department of Archaeology at Cairo University, treated the coins with chemicals to remove the rust. He previously supervised the conservation of the Twenty-sixth Dynasty tombs and temples at the Oasis (see chapter 14).

One of the most unique and best-preserved artifacts we found is a completely intact wooden panel carved and painted with a scene that depicts one of the mummies standing in the center as a statue of the crowned Osiris. On either side of him stand the gods Horus and Anubis, and next to them are two cobras to protect the deceased on his journey. The scene is framed by two painted columns, which represent the primordial mound out of which all life originally sprang. Across the top of the panel are three levels of the image most commonly found at the top of tomb entrances, the sun disk. The entire scene is meant to confirm the fate of the deceased as that of Osiris, risen into eternity, a smaller version of what would normally be carved or painted on the walls of a tomb by expensive artisans. Perhaps because desert sandstone crumbles so easily and would not maintain such wall carvings for very long, this wood panel served the same function, to insure the safe passage of the deceased into the afterlife.

# MR. X GOES TO GIZA

At THE END OF THE EXCAVATION SEASON IN 1999, WE DECIDED TO REMOVE a mummy from one of the tombs at Bahariya Oasis and transfer it to our on-site conservation tent for treatment before sending it to Giza for X rays. I had asked that an X-ray machine be brought from our osteological laboratory at Giza so that we could conduct extensive tests on various mummies without moving them too far from their families in the tombs and return them to their resting places as soon as possible. However, Dr. Azza Sarry el-Din, physical anthropologist for the National Research Center in charge of X-raying skeletal remains at Giza sites, informed me that too much sand could do the machine serious damage. Because it is the only X-ray machine we have at the site of the Tombs of the Pyramid Builders, we agreed that it was too risky to use it on-site at Bahariya. We would have to choose one of the mummies and send it to Cairo for examination.

Bones alone can tell many stories. X rays of mummy skeletons have proved to be an invaluable, noninvasive tool for ascertaining causes of death and types of diseases suffered by ancient Egyptians in certain periods, as well as information about deformities and even ancient dentistry practices. This area of archaeology is a relatively new field known as paleopathology, the study of ancient diseases. As early as 1896, the newly invented X-ray machine was used on mummies, but mainly for the purpose of locating amulets and jewelry without unwrapping bodies and thus destroying them. More recently, the archaeologists Kent Weeks of the American University in Cairo, Edward Wente of the Oriental Institute in Chicago, and James Harris of the University of Michigan's Dentistry Department led a comprehensive X-ray investigation of the royal mummies at the Egyptian Museum in Cairo. Thanks to their work, we now know which kings suffered from abscesses and arthritis, the two most prevalent health problems of ancient royalty. X rays of the mummy of Tutankhamun revealing damage to the back of his skull have led to a much-debated theory that the famous young ruler was murdered. From examinations completed in the laboratory at Giza of the skeletons found by my team in the Tombs of the Pyramid Builders, I was able to corroborate my own theory that the tombs did, in fact, belong to the builders of the pyramids, for X rays show severe degenerative joint diseases, particularly in the lumbar region of the spine and knees, characteristic of rigorous activity and the lifting of heavy objects.

New technology more recently applied to archaeological studies, such as DNA testing and CAT scans, has added an entirely new dimension to our ability to learn from mummies. For example, family relationships within the royal dynasties suggested by archaeological evidence can now be confirmed through DNA samples of teeth, hair, or fingernails. DNA tests have also been conducted on ancient Egyptians to determine their ethnic makeup, although so far such work has been inconclusive. In the case of the golden mummies of Bahariya, DNA testing could potentially be applied to trace Greek, Roman, and Egyptian lineage and to give us a more precise

picture of who the inhabitants of the Bahariya Oasis were, exactly when they lived there, and the evolution of diseases during this period.

A few days before our team closed the excavation site for the season, I selected for testing a mummy wrapped in linen rather than one covered in gold or cartonnage, so that it could be more easily transported and X-rayed. It was found alone in a shaft inside Tomb 55, and we did not have to disturb any other mummies during the removal process. This mummy is one of my favorites, because it is in excellent condition and thus reminds me of New Kingdom mummies. Considering the way in which the mummy was buried, the deceased must have been relatively poor, which also endeared it to me.

After I pointed out the mummy to my colleagues Nasry Iskander and Moustafa Abdul Qader, they set to work doing the necessary conservation. They painstakingly applied a chemical to the outer layer of linen to make it strong enough to withstand unraveling or tearing. This process, called consolidation, was completed in situ, and the mummy could not be moved until it was dry, which took almost two days. Meanwhile, a carpenter prepared a wooden box that would fit the mummy's exact proportions. We bought cotton and other soft materials to serve as bedding and then erected a tent as the mummy's temporary home during further conservation.

The next step was to extricate the mummy from its resting place. Nasry Iskander put a very thin wooden tray under the body and then very carefully lifted it into the new coffin. I overheard Mansour Boriak asking Moustafa why we had chosen this particular mummy, when one of the gilded ones would be received as royalty in Cairo. Moustafa reminded him that this simple example was less likely to be damaged. Mansour lit a cigarette and shook his head, saying, "I just hope he likes to travel. If not, our days are black." Moustafa said, "You mean 'the curse'?" Mansour nodded. (For more on the curse of the mummies, see the next chapter.)

Mummies elicit this inexplicable effect in nearly everyone, even the scientifically minded. Mohammed Tiyab, who is a native of Bahariya, spoke sadly of the possibility that this mummy might be one of his ancestors, something he would never know. Many questions were arising in my mind as well: Did he or she ever visit the pyramids before this? Is he or she happy or unhappy about leaving home for a strange new place? Why did I really choose this one instead of another? I had no answers.

We were all concerned that the mummy might be damaged on the way to Cairo by the violent movement of a truck traveling more than two hundred miles on a semipaved road, so it stayed in the tent for three more days while more consolidation was done. The day we were to leave, Mansour came to me with an urgent question. "Doctor! What will we name it? Does it already have a name?" No, I realized, it didn't. Unlike ancient Egyptian burials,

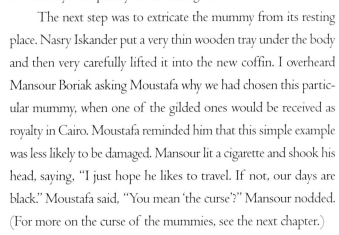

The mummy of Mr. X being lifted out of the burial chamber

*Left:* Mr. X lies in his new wooden coffin wrapped in one continuous sheet of linen, which was tied in horizontal strips across his body.

*Opposite top:* The mummy of one of the sons of Ramses II, King Merenptah, now in the Egyptian Museum in Cairo, was one of the royal mummies to undergo X-ray examinations.

*Opposite bottom:* Tomb 55, with four burial chambers and a niche also used for burial

*Page 80:* Mr. X, as he was found in Tomb 55

where cartouches and wall inscriptions in the tombs provide the names of the deceased, mass graves from Greco-Roman times contain no records of anyone's identity. The mummy from Bahariya needed to acquire some sort of identity before it left. Because of its as yet undetermined gender, I chose to call it "Mr. or Mrs. X." On the last day of our excavation and conservation work, we prepared the truck for the mummy's departure. No one said a word as the movers lifted the box up onto their shoulders and into the back of the truck. Everyone on the site was quiet. I wondered if the deceased, in life, ever imagined that his or her mummy would one day be carried out of the cemetery just as it had been carried in.

The workmen look on as Mr. X sees the light of day for the first time in almost 2,000 years

*Right:* Moustafa Abdul Qader guides Mr. X to the conservation tent to be prepared for his trip to Giza.

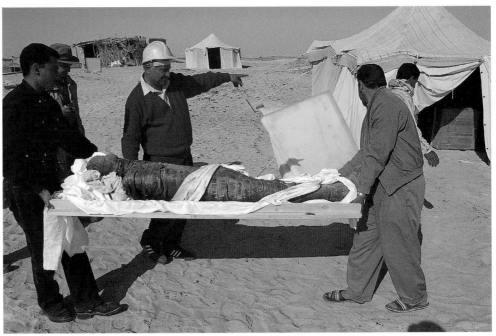

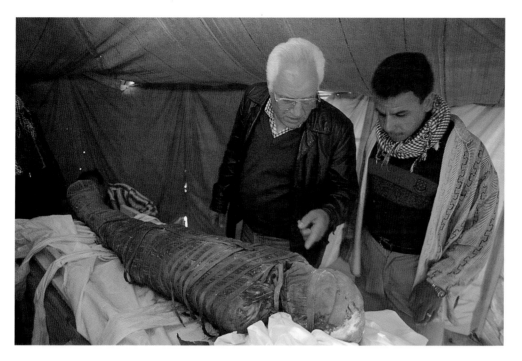

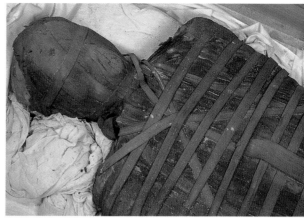

Mr. X awaits his departure to Giza, where he will undergo X-ray examination. The linen on his head and chest is black from resin.

*Left:* Conservator Nasry Iskander inspects the condition of the elaborately wrapped mummy.

*Below left:* After conservation, Mr. X was carried to the truck.

*Bottom:* The wooden coffin is lifted into the truck for the drive to Giza.

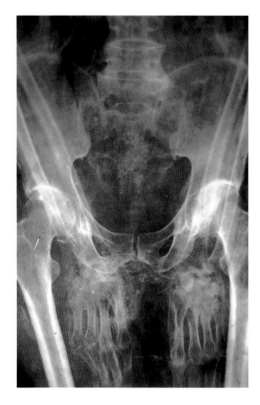

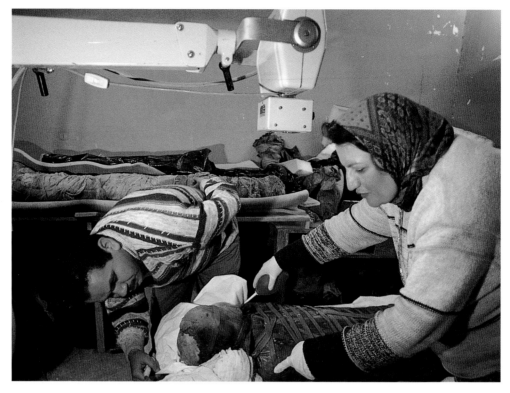

Mr. X as seen by scientists in the osteological laboratory at Giza

*Above right:* Anthropologist Azza Sarry el-Din dries the chemicals used to prepare Mr. X for examination.

*Below:* Dr. Azza studies the results of X-ray examinations conducted on Mr. X.

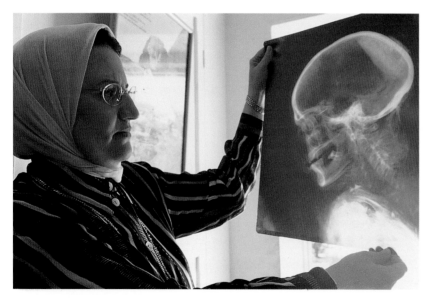

At first I decided to ride in the truck with the mummy, because we were afraid that if the police stopped and searched the truck, they would assume we had stolen a dead body. But I needed to finish up the work at the Oasis, so I asked Mahmoud Afifi if he would escort the mummy to Cairo. I wrote a letter that he could show to anyone who might wonder what was happening, stating that this mummy came from our excavation site and was traveling to Cairo for X rays. Our situation reminded me of the stories told about the removal and subsequent transport to Cairo of the royal mummies found in the cache at Deir el-Bahri in 1881. As the ships passed carrying the mummies, the men of the West Bank ran to the shore of the Nile accompanied by women dressed in black, who wept as if their own family members had died. Later, when the mummies were received in Cairo, a customs officer insisted they be taxed as cargo, but since there was no established category of cargo called "mummy," the officer had the royal mummies taxed as salted fish! I hoped our mummy would not have to suffer any such indignity. To avoid this, we sent official messages to all the local police from Bahariya to Cairo, informing them of the departure of the mummy for the pyramids. In addition, my office assistant at the Giza Plateau arranged for everyone there to receive Mr. or Mrs. X with respect. During the entire process I was struck by the care and regard that everyone gave to the mummy. Even though this person had died long ago, I think it is natural that we felt a kinship, recognizing that this could be our own fate someday. So we always treat a mummy as if it were still a person, just as we would hope to be treated ourselves in similar circumstances.

The trip from Bahariya to Giza, which normally takes three to four hours, took our driver eight, as he carefully avoided potholes and other hazards. By evening the truck was parked in front of the pyramids, where it was guarded until the next morning, when I met Dr. Azza in the osteology lab. It took only two hours for her to make this report:

Sex: Male

Age at death: 35 to 40

Pathology: None

Name: Mr. X

The results also showed that two molars had been extracted from the mandible, which indicates that dentistry was still actively practiced during the Greco-Roman Period. We expect that Mr. X will provide much more valuable information as scientists continue to study him and others from the Valley of the Golden Mummies.

After this episode, I decided to acquire an X-ray machine for the Bahariya site in order to carry on further studies there, although it still had not arrived as of this writing. In the meantime, I include here the research of Teri L. Tucker, an American Research Center Fellow from Ohio State University, to whom I gave permission to examine skeletal material from six tombs found in

Bones are removed from the Valley of the Golden Mummies for skeletal studies.

Bones are sifted to be used for skeletal analysis in order to eliminate pieces of dried mud, stones, and leaves.

Bahariya in 1996. With Mohammed Aiady as her Antiquities Inspector, Tucker began the study in 1998 to test her theory that, despite the commonly held belief that centralized economic and political authority improve the standard of living for citizens, the opposite may in fact be true—that a society's quality of life and therefore health improve more effectively when people have autonomy. Both health and the overall quality of life can be measured by indicators of stress in the bones. By recording the rate of such factors as infant mortality, average life expectancy, infectious diseases, broken bones, dental conditions, and other factors in mummies from both Giza and Bahariya and then comparing the results, Tucker hoped to gain a better understanding of the effect of Roman rule on the people of the Nile Valley, as opposed to the more remote and therefore more self-sufficient people of Bahariya Oasis. She expected to find that, as strict economic control became more centralized in the Nile Valley during the Greco-Roman Period, there would be a noticeable increase in problems caused by poor diet, high rates of disease, and bone trauma. By the same token, little or no increase of these problems should be evident in the Bahariya population, who were presumably more autonomous.

From tombs found at different sites at Bahariya, Tucker examined bone samples from 167 men, women, and children for her study. She collected skeletal data relating to age, gender, ancestry, skeletal lesions with signs of infection, long-bone growth rates, adult height, sexual dimorphism, tooth decay, and evidence of trauma, metabolic disease, cranial deformation, or other disorders. The results of her investigation indicated that the average age at death was as low as twenty-five to thirty-five years. Although about half of the population of ancient Egypt died during infancy or childhood, usually because of infectious disease, there was little evidence of such diseases in Bahariya. There was, however, a high rate of osteoarthritis, which usually appeared before the age of thirty, the result of habitual movement, a reflection of daily activity. Interestingly, 71 percent of the women and 44 percent of the men show facets on the distal tibia, a common result of squatting. Other pathologies she observed included spina bifida and bone fractures, but there is little evidence that the fractures were caused by violence at the hands of the Roman masters; most of them can be attributed to accidents.

Untreated tooth infections resulted in death 50 to 90 percent of the time in ancient Egypt, but people of Bahariya Oasis suffered relatively few dental problems, perhaps because their diet was largely made up of wheat, which scours the surface of the teeth and prevents the buildup of harmful bacteria that cause cavities. It is also assumed that the people of Bahariya Oasis enjoyed a healthy diet, including the iron-rich dates that were abundant in that region. The specimens from certain Bahariya tombs reflected a high rate of cribia orbitalia and enamel defects, while other groups were minimally affected. Tucker believes this suggests that some of the individuals enjoyed an elite status and had access to better food resources. However, further research must still be done.

Tucker's extensive X-ray examinations thus enabled her to conclude that the people of Bahariya were unlikely to have been harshly treated by the Roman presence. In fact, despite their low life expectancy, this tomb's population actually lived longer than the average Egyptian in the Nile Valley during Roman rule. Tucker's investigation to date has not revealed why the Oasis population appears to have declined dramatically during the fifth and sixth centuries A.D., but her research indicates that this was not the result of infectious disease. She plans to continue these bone studies to test her theories further, and we trust that more valuable information will be forthcoming about the way in which the inhabitants of Bahariya Oasis lived, as well as died.

In the near future, we hope to complete DNA analyses of the mummies from the Valley of the Golden Mummies to unlock the mystery of the exact genealogical ancestry of the population of Bahariya during the time the cemetery was in active use. In the same way that DNA from the mummies was used to determine the identity of the royal mummies at the Cairo Museum, it may also confirm the archaeological and historical evidence that Bahariya was inhabited by Libyans, Egyptians, Greeks, and Romans during this time. Eventually, we hope that DNA evidence of the people of old Bahariya can be compared with that from the other oases and the Nile Valley and can help explain the ancestral relationship of those peoples. These ambitious projects are good examples of the wide range of conclusions that we may be able to draw from the scientific data derived from the golden mummies.

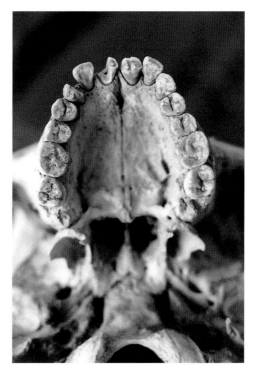

**A jaw from a Bahariya skull used in X-ray studies conducted by Teri Tucker to analyze dental problems**

# THE CURSE OF
# THE CHILD MUMMIES

AFTER I MADE AN OFFICIAL ANNOUNCEMENT OF THE DISCOVERY IN JUNE 1999, the Minister of Culture, Farouk Hosni, and the General Secretary of the Antiquities Department, Dr. Gaballa Ali Gaballa, released the news to the press. Little did I know that the everyday work of the excavation was nothing compared to what was in store for us. Friends from Egypt and America, news teams from Europe, tourist companies, professors, ambassadors from Australia, the Czech Republic, Italy, and the United States—they all came to the little town of El Bawiti to visit the site before we had prepared any policy on public viewing.

By the end of the first season in 1999, I was being pressured, or strongly encouraged, to open up the site to tourists, not only by people who had heard about the discovery and were eager to see the spectacular site, but also by tourist agents who wanted to design tours around the golden mummies. The most enthusiastic response, however, came from the Egyptian government, which, of course, is supported to a great extent by our tourism industry. Because I do not like the idea of masses of people tromping through the cemetery, I conceded instead to delivering at least five of the best-preserved mummies to a room in the Inspectorate of Antiquities, which was then being converted into the Bahariya Museum.

It never occurred to me until I moved the two children to their resting place in the Bahariya Museum that the so-called curse of the mummies existed. The idea of a curse connected with mummies has been around since the excavation of the tomb of Tutankhamun by Howard Carter and Lord Carnarvon in 1922. It was claimed in newspapers all over the world that several people who had taken part in the discovery had died soon after the pharaoh's burial chamber was opened. The benefactor Lord Carnarvon, who demanded half the artifacts and sold the exclusive rights to publish anything about the tomb to the *Times* of London, died one year after the discovery, on May 6, 1923. The lights in Cairo were reported to have blacked out at the moment of his death. Even Lord Carnarvon's son, Lord Porchester, added to the mystery by recounting that his father's dog, at home in the family castle in England, let out a pitiful cry at the moment of his master's death and then died himself. Reputable newspapers all over the world reported that mysterious, ominous forces unleashed from the tomb were the cause of as many as twenty-two deaths. Of the twelve people who had witnessed the opening of the sarcophagus, six died by the following February. Even Howard Carter was ousted from the site and suffered psychologically for many years from all the pressure and politics and from being banned from his site. Many people believed it was because their actions had offended the ancient Egyptian king. The papers even reworked a translation of a text inscribed on the wall in front of the Anubis shrine in the tomb's treasury to

The girl mummy on her way to the conservation tent to be prepared for her removal to the Bahariya Museum

*Below:* The boy mummy is uncovered.

*Page 90:* The girl mummy is one of those rare mummies who seem to be smiling.

say: "I am the one who prevents the sand from blocking the secret chamber. I will kill all those who cross this threshold into the sacred precincts of the royal king who lives forever."

David Silverman, curator of the Egyptian Department at the University of Pennsylvania Museum, was also the curator at the Field Museum of the Tutankhamun exhibition when it stopped in Chicago on its world tour. In an article about the incident, he wrote that the electricity goes out frequently in Cairo and that Carnarvon's son was actually in India at the time of his father's death. Lord Carnarvon had been very sick the last few years of the excavation and died of blood poisoning from a mosquito bite on his cheek that was cut open while shaving.

During the last hundred years, the clichéd "curse of the pharaoh" has been used to explain the cause of death in all sorts of unrelated incidents. Other deaths somberly tallied even include that of Jean-François Champollion, the French archaeologist who translated hieroglyphics on the

Moustafa Abdul Qader and the author take one last look at the mummy of the little girl before she is removed from the site.

*Below:* Mansour Boriak and the author take measurements of the children.

*Below right:* After wrapping the lower half of the boy's body in cotton, the conservator prepares the boy for his journey to the museum.

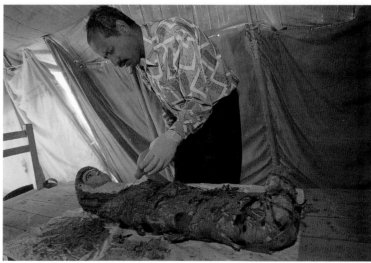

basis of the Rosetta Stone and happened to die at the early age of forty-two. Shortly after the Director of Antiquities Mohammed Mahdy signed a contract for Tutankhamun's funerary objects to be exhibited in London, he was killed in an automobile accident. The author of a book entitled *The Curse* relates that he later asked the Director of Antiquities Dr. Gamal Mehrez, if he believed in the curse, to which the scholar replied, "I have excavated tombs and mummies and nothing happened to me." The writer adds that Dr. Mehrez died the very next day. What he fails to point out was that Dr. Mehrez was an Islamic scholar who had never excavated anything related to pharaonic Egypt and that he was already suffering with health problems from which he was expected to die.

In most cases, reasonable explanations can readily be found, but it is true that verses inscribed on the entrances of ancient Egyptian tombs have the sole purpose of deliberately frightening anyone from entering and disturbing the souls of those who are buried there. For example: "Cursed be those that disturb the rest of the pharaoh. They that shall break the seal of this tomb shall meet death by a disease that no doctor can diagnose."

The ancient Egyptians had a strong belief in magic, but most of these curses were simply threats left behind by private citizens, especially during the Old Kingdom, in the hope that the graves of their loved ones would not be vandalized. One common curse went: "As for anyone who will do something evil against my grave, remove any stone or any brick from this my tomb, enter my tomb, enter this tomb in my purity, seize a stone from this my tomb, enter upon these my images in my purity, he will be judged regarding it by the great god. I will wring his neck like a goose or a bird and cause those who live up on earth to fear the spirits who are in the west. I will exterminate his survivors. I will not allow their forms to be occupied." Even private letters contained expressions of ill will. One letter collected by Silverman, written by a woman of the Middle Kingdom, says: "May you be sick when you read this."

Members of the royal family had their own protection in the form of strongly constructed or hidden tombs with labyrinthine corridors and false doors. Their spells, called *Pyramid Texts*, were meant to insure the success of their own treacherous journey through the underworld, and as Silverman relates, the royal curses, when they did occur, were more directed at the difficulties on the way to eternity than they were intended as a protection against vandals. In Deir el-Bahri, Thutmose I addresses the court of his daughter, the reigning pharaoh Hatshepsut: "He who will adore her, he will live. He who will speak evil in a curse against her majesty, he will die."

At the beginning of my career, during my first year excavating at Kom Abu-Bellou in the Nile Delta, I had to remove a truckload of gold objects and other artifacts from a Greco-Roman cemetery and transport them to the Egyptian Museum in Cairo. That same day, my cousin died. Two years later on the anniversary of that day, my uncle died. On the same day of the third year, my aunt died. It seemed a strange coincidence at the time, but being young, I didn't think much about it. I admit that I never shave on the day we are to open a new tomb, but this is not superstition. It is precaution against the active bacteria from deteriorating organic material that can enter any open wound on the skin and pose the risk of death.

Years later, when I was excavating at the Tombs of the Pyramid Builders at Giza, we came across a text on the entrance to a tomb: "O all people who enter this tomb, who will make evil

The boy mummy wears a Greco-Roman type of head-band decorated with leaves and flowers.

Below: A conservator wears a mask to protect himself against active bacteria that may be released as he brushes sand away from the deteriorating organic material of the mummy.

against this tomb and destroy it, may the crocodile be against them on water, and snakes against them on land. May the hippopotamus be against them on water, the scorpion against them on land."

This was the first curse I had come across on an undisturbed tomb, and it convinced me to preserve every aspect of the site and not to disturb the mummies within. It was not until I began working in Bahariya Oasis, when we had to remove two of the child mummies to the museum, that I began to wonder if there wasn't some truth to the tradition.

I watched as Moustafa Abdul Qader and Salah Ahmed Ali covered the lower half of the children's bodies with linen before lifting them from their places next to each other on the mastaba. The men wore masks over their mouths to guard against any bacterial diseases. They first carefully placed two sticks under each mummy, lifted both into two separate coffins, and carried them to a waiting truck. The whole process took two hours. I was

content that the two siblings would be able to stay together, so I left to join the group for dinner, and we enjoyed ourselves, knowing that our work would soon end for the season.

I could not sleep that night. Whenever I closed my eyes, the faces of the children appeared and would not go away. I sat up several times and opened my eyes in an effort to dismiss them. Finally I fell asleep exhausted and had a nightmare. They would not stop following me in my dream, wherever I turned. Although they were still wrapped like babies in the fresh linen we had given them, their arms began to stretch out and grab at me. Then I saw the smiling face of Mummy B, the woman we had also taken to the museum, but her eyes were pleading with me. She was trying to tell me something but I could not understand.

Soon afterward, we returned to Cairo, and I had to prepare quickly to move to Los Angeles for the summer to teach at UCLA, which I have done for the past five years. It is normally very peaceful there, and I use the time to write articles in my rented apartment in Marina del Rey. Not only did the children follow me to America to haunt my dreams this time, but the interest prompted by the public announcement of the discovery had also caught on like wildfire. After the editors of *Archaeology Magazine*, Peter Young and Mark Rose, did a cover article on me called "The Prince of the Pyramids," photographs of the golden mummies appeared on front pages all over the world. Suddenly I was being asked to do television and magazine interviews almost every day between classes. Meanwhile, I was losing sleep from nightmares. On the evening I did an interview about the Valley of the Golden Mummies for *CNN Live,* I was so disturbed by my nightmares that I almost talked about them on international television.

Then one night the children came to me again in my sleep. This time the little girl started to stretch her long arms toward my throat. I got up screaming. I had to wake up at 4:00 A.M. and get to the airport by 5:00 to catch a flight to Virginia, where I was to give a lecture on the golden mummies at 7:00 P.M. at the Richmond Art Museum. I waited for the taxi outside my building until 5:00, but it never came. I was already nervous, but I finally managed to find another cab and make the flight at the last minute. I arrived in Philadelphia for my connecting flight to Richmond, only to discover that it had been canceled. All I could think about were the five hundred people waiting to hear me speak and those little hands reaching for my neck. After I explained the problem to the airline personnel, they put me on a flight that would arrive at 5:30 P.M. in New Williamsport, where a taxi to Richmond would only take an hour. We landed at 6:00, and the taxi immediately got stuck in traffic. I could hardly breathe, I was in such a panic. It was as if that little girl had her hands around my throat. The driver assured me he knew the city well and how to get to the museum. We arrived in Richmond at 7:30, and he began to stop to ask people for directions.

When we finally pulled up at the museum, I ran in, apologized to the director, and explained what had happened. A full auditorium was waiting to hear all about the mummies, but I was badly in need of a change of clothes and a shave, so I ran to a bathroom and took off all my clothes, only to find that there was no running water. I got dressed again and was directed to another bathroom. I finally gave my lecture at 9:00 and found myself telling the crowd about the curse of the mummies, although I did not mention the children or my nightmares.

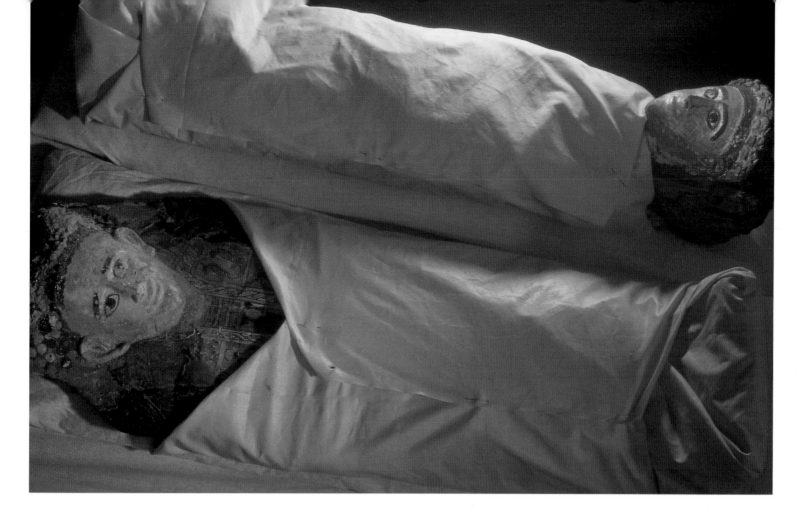

At dinner that night with the museum's director and her husband, she reminded me that I had agreed to give a lecture to a group of schoolteachers the next morning at 9:00. I set my wake-up call that night for 8:00 A.M. and then left the phone off the hook, so after an unrestful night, I woke up to people knocking on my door at 9:30. I could not ignore the children anymore. At the Richmond Airport that morning, I took the time to concentrate on the day we had moved the mummies of the children to the Bahariya Museum. I recalled every detail of their fresh, golden faces and dark, shining eyes as they were lifted into their newly made coffins. One minute before my flight was called, I said to myself: "I know why the children are upset. They need to have their father with them." I promised myself that when I returned to Egypt, I would go to Bahariya and move their father to the museum.

At the end of September 1999, I went to Bahariya again and took Salah Ahmed Ali, the conservator, Ashry Shaker, and Mohammed Aiady back to the site to move the father to the museum. The children never came into my dreams again. I still believe that mummies should not be displayed, but this is a compromise that I consider better than allowing tourists into the burial site itself. In a way I guess those six mummies are making a sacrifice for the rest of their colleagues at the site in order to restore this vision of our past.

There must be a reason why mummies and tales of a distant past still resonate in our modern world. The people buried here seem to speak to us from their graves, and I believe it can serve our own society if we listen to them. As we continue the excavation next season, they will tell us many stories of a great civilization, and their stories will live on in us. I want to give them this opportunity, for perhaps then, in one sense, they will have achieved eternal life after all.

**The boy and girl mummies lying together in the Bahariya Museum.**

*Opposite top:* A workman cleans sand from the father of the child mummies.

*Opposite bottom:* Nasry Iskander prepares the father mummy for his transport to the museum to be with his two children.

# PART II
# EGYPT—ANCIENT TO GRECO-ROMAN

# BAHARIYA OASIS: PAST AND PRESENT

MILLIONS OF YEARS AGO, WHAT IS NOW CALLED THE WESTERN (OR Libyan) Desert was the floor of an immense ocean. Since about 3000 B.C., this part of the Sahara has experienced almost no rainfall, yet enough groundwater exists beneath the surface to have been the source of five major oases. Geologists cannot explain the origin of this water, nor can they tell how much there is, although there is clear evidence that the supply has diminished considerably over the years. The oases include Bahariya, Kharga, Dakhla, Farafra (the largest in size), and Siwa (the largest in population). Bahariya, sometimes referred to as the Northern Oasis, is located approximately 260 miles southwest of Cairo. The oasis is actually a large oval depression about 1,240 square miles in size, surrounded with mountains and comprising hundreds of springs around which villages have developed over the millennia. The area is rich in iron deposits, and the availability of water has made the earth capable of producing grapes, dates, and other produce.

Remains of stone tools found in Bahariya Oasis indicate that the area was settled as early as the Paleolithic Period. In fact, anyone with a trained eye who walks around Bahariya's sites can spot prehistoric stone knives and hand axes simply lying on the surface of the sand. Further south in the desert, in Wadi el-Ewinat and Darb el-Shobary, which lie between Dakhla and Kharga Oases, and in the Kharga towns of Gebel and Eltier, rock drawings made with primitive tools have been dated as early as 4000 B.C. During the First Dynasty of the Early Dynastic Period (3100–2686 B.C.), the rulers of Egypt fought with a people known as the Tjehenu, who lived in the Western Desert and who are depicted in ancient art as fair-skinned with blond hair and blue eyes. The people who ultimately settled in Bahariya Oasis were a mix of people from the Nile Valley and Bedouins from Libya.

We have not yet been able to conclude where the earliest inhabitants of Bahariya Oasis actually lived, because a thorough survey of the area has not been carried out. Settlement sites dated to the Predynastic, Early Dynastic, and Old Kingdom Periods have yet to be found in Bahariya, although they have been located in Dakhla and Kharga. My guess is that there was an early settlement at or near the site of the modern town of El Bawiti, but the range of ruins throughout Bahariya suggests that the water level—and hence the area available for cultivation—was once substantially wider than it is today.

We still have not found any evidence of human civilization in this region dating to the Old Kingdom (2686–2181 B.C.). In fact, it was not until the Middle Kingdom that the area is documented as being under official Egyptian jurisdiction. Records from this period refer to the intersection at Bahariya of two major trade routes along which wine and other products were exported from the oases to the Nile Valley. One of the routes connected directly to Bahnasa, and the other

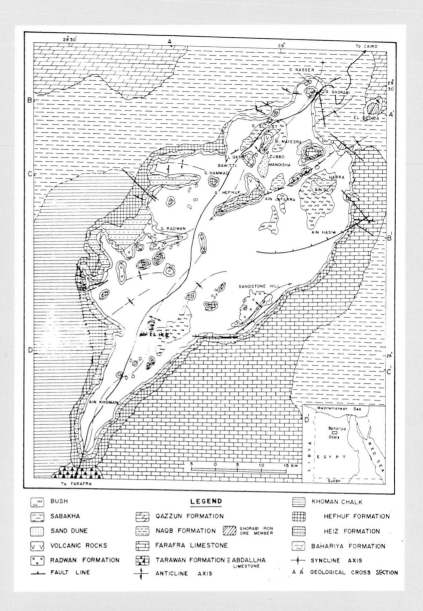

**Geological map of Bahariya Oasis**

*Left:* Bahariya Oasis, as seen from the iron-rich black mountains to the west

*Page 100:* A farmer returns home on his donkey after a long day of work.

*Pages 98–99:* The wind formed the spectacular rock shapes in the White Desert about forty miles south of El Bawiti.

Modern farms in El Bawiti, the capital of Bahariya Oasis; the ancient capital was located at El Qasr, a nearby village.

to the pyramids at Giza. These ancient caravan routes are still in use today, having been paved only about twenty years ago.

The only documented artifact from the area dating to the Middle Kingdom is a scarab, found near El Bawiti during the 1930s by the Egyptian archaeologist Ahmed Fakhry, inscribed with the name of Senusret, one of three pharaohs of the Twelfth Dynasty with the same name. Historic records show that the pharaohs Amenemhet and Senusret II began to pay attention to the borders of the western oases in order to divert regular attacks from the Libyans. During the Fifteenth Dynasty (1650–1550 B.C.), a transitional period, when Egypt was ruled by the Hyksos kings from Palestine, there was a lapse in trade with the Oasis, largely because the roads were unsafe. Only one text survives from this time, in which the Egyptian King Kamose refers to Bahariya as DjesDjes, the word for the region's famous wine.

On the basis of archaeological and historical records, we know that Bahariya Oasis experienced significant changes during the Eighteenth Dynasty (1550–1295 B.C.) of the New Kingdom. The oldest tomb yet found there is that of Amenhotep Huy, who held the title "Governor of the Northern Oasis." Officials had been sent to govern Bahariya in accordance with a decree of Thutmose III (r. 1479–1425 B.C.), perhaps because he recognized the Oasis's importance in defending Egypt's western borders. It was during this time that residents began to worship Egyptian gods, probably imported with settlers from the Nile Valley. In all likelihood, however, these officials preferred to live in the Nile Valley, where the pharaoh ruled, and about 125 years after Thutmose's decree, Amenhotep Huy, a native of Bahariya, was appointed to serve as the local administrator. The inhabitants of Bahariya must have begun by this time to mine and trade iron ore and other mineral deposits found in the area, because there is evidence of their use throughout the rest of Egypt. Unlike residents of the Nile Valley, who depended on the seasonal variations in the Nile's water level, the people of the oases enjoyed the constant availability of a controlled supply of water, thanks to their artesian-well system. They grew abundant produce on their farms, including dates, grapes, and figs, and raised livestock and pigeons.

In the Temple of Amun at Luxor, the great pharaoh Ramses II of the Nineteenth Dynasty referred to Bahariya as a place of mining. During the reign of his son Merenptah, Egypt was again attacked by Libyan forces, and several references have been found on temple stelae and pylons of this time to Bahariya and Farafra Oases, which must have suffered during the constant border wars. Ramses III of the Twentieth Dynasty also fought the Libyans, whom he defeated and brought back to Egypt as slaves, after which Bahariya returned to its earlier level of productivity and began

**El Bawiti today**

to produce wine for export. In the Great Harris Papyrus (in the British Museum), which includes a list of the temple endowments and achievements of Ramses III, the king makes a reference to Bahariya's wine by saying that he wished the wine of the northern oasis were like that of the southern oasis (presumably Kharga).

During the Twenty-first Dynasty, following the weak reign of Ramses XI, the Libyans who had been forced to settle in Egypt became gradually more powerful and eventually took control of Thebes to rule Egypt for nearly three centuries. The Libyan rulers of the Twenty-second Dynasty deemed Kharga, Dakhla, and Bahariya Oases of strategic importance. Funerary stelae, found in an unfinished sandstone chapel at the site of El Eion (in El Bawiti), originally thought to be dated to the reign of Thutmose II (1492–1479 B.C.), have since been reexamined and found to belong to the Libyan ruler Sheshonq IV (r. c. 780 B.C.), based on examples found in the chapel's entrance with the latter's name inscribed in a cartouche. More evidence dating to the reign of this king indicates that Bahariya Oasis was under the control of a government official named Weshet-het, who held the title "Superior Lybian Chief." Another Libyan, known as Arcawa, became governor and priest of Bahariya at the end of the Twenty-second Dynasty; he and his family were responsible for the construction of monuments at that time.

It was not until after Egypt had been reunified under the Twenty-fifth (Kushite) and Twenty-

**Beyond the dunes and farms of El Bawiti lie the sandstone remains of the Temple of Alexander the Great.**

sixth (Saite) Dynasties, which put an end to Libyan rule, that Bahariya flourished as an important agricultural and trade center with its own administrators. Soldiers and officials were sent to live in Bahariya, which was governed from Abydos, near Thebes. Documents now in the Louvre suggest that an individual named Antef of Abydos served as governor of all the oases. More wells were dug and farms were expanded; many Egyptians moved to the Oasis to live and work there, and we have found many of their tombs dating from this period.

There was, during the sixth century B.C., a power struggle between the king, Apries (r. 589–570 B.C.), and Ahmose, the head of the Egyptian army, who sent troops to the Western Desert, where he victoriously defended Egyptian interests against the Greeks and Libyans. Ahmose was subsequently crowned as Ahmose II (r. 570–526 B.C.). He fully understood the importance of Bahariya as the gateway to Egypt from the west and protected it vigilantly against attacks from then on. To honor this, two temples and many chapels near Ain el-Muftella (an ancient site near El Bawiti) were erected in his name by the second priest of Bahariya, Wah-ibranefer, the son of Arknakht, under the supervision of Prince Sotekh-erdies, who appears in a scene on the temple walls with a feather on his head. His grandson Zed-Khonsu-efankh would later make additions to the temples of Ahmose (see chapter 14 for more about these sites).

After a series of hostile takeovers during the Late Period by the Nubians and the Assyrians, Egypt was annexed into the Persian Empire in the Twenty-seventh Dynasty. A strong military presence and garrison were established in Bahariya, and more rooms and chapels were added to the temples of Ahmose. Still, this could not stop the Macedonian conqueror, Alexander the Great, from eventually taking control of Egypt and its oases in 332 B.C. In fact, Alexander was a welcome liberator of Egyptians from Persian rule. After he made his famous journey to the Siwa Oasis to be recognized as the divine pharaoh of Egypt by the oracle of Amun, he or one of his followers may have taken the connecting route to Bahariya, because it is here that we find the only temple dedicated to Alexander in all of Egypt.

**The sandstone sanctuary of the Temple of Alexander the Great**

Alexander and Ptolemy, commander of the Egyptian army and Alexander's successor, organized Egypt under a centrally controlled government to profit Greece, and Bahariya began to thrive during the economic resurgence that followed. Trade routes developed through the oases, especially to Libya, and more military outposts were set up, this time not only to protect Bahariya from outside attack, but also to establish a place from which the Greek rulers of Egypt, called the Ptolemies, could take control of the rest of the Western Desert, which they eventually did. After the Ptolemaic kings captured Libya, they constructed a strong military garrison in Bahariya to protect the trade routes between Egypt and Darfur via the Darb el-Arba'in trail, or the "Forty Days Road," which connected Kharga Oasis with western Sudan.

The archaeologists Georg Steindorff and Ahmed Fakhry recorded various mud-brick structures built by the Ptolemies near El Bawiti, but these have yet to be fully uncovered, although the Antiquities Department has scheduled their complete excavation for the near future. On the entrances and walls of these structures are depictions of Thoth as an ibis and inscriptions—some still in traditional hieratic script and some in the more recent demotic script—which will make this site one of great interest to scholars of Greco-Roman Egypt. In various temples in Egypt dated from the Ptolemaic Period, the goddess Hathor is referred to as "Lady of Bahariya Oasis," while Khonsu, the moon-god, and Amun were called "Lords of Bahariya Oasis." Amun was the

Inside the Temple of Alexander the Great, the author sits next to archaeologist Tohfa Handussa, while Shafia Bedeer examines the Coptic graffiti left behind by ancient visitors to the temple.

most important central god in the Oasis at this time, which is why Alexander the Great dedicated his temple to him. I have concluded that the cemetery containing the golden mummies, which exemplify the wealth that the locals accumulated during this time, was established near the Temple of Alexander the Great during his reign, about 332 B.C.

The culture and economy of Bahariya must have declined temporarily as the Ptolemaic government battled the Romans for control of the Oasis. Research shows, for example, that the Oasis irrigation systems were expanded by the first Ptolemies but then fell into disrepair under the last Greek rulers. Under the Romans, however, Bahariya Oasis flourished again, possibly even more than it had during the high points of the Eighteenth and Twenty-sixth Dynasties. Roman rule brought about increased revenue from massive grain exports to Rome, as well as new public-works projects. Pottery dating from Roman times was also found on a site called Ain el-Siwi, known today as Ain el-Geblia. This cluster of mud-brick houses and a cemetery south of the dwellings formed an agricultural settlement outside the ancient Bahariya capital of El Qasr (close to El Bawiti). The site of El Qasr itself provides evidence of houses, churches, and another cemetery dating from the second century A.D. There the most important Roman symbol of victory, an arch, was left behind.

In Bahariya more roads were cut, ancient wells and aqueducts were restored and improved, and thousands of mud-brick buildings were constructed. This rapid growth and increased wealth

In the fading sunlight, archaeologists examine inscriptions on the Temple of Alexander the Great.

continued until the third century A.D. Under the floor of a house in the small village of El Meysera, Fakhry found a vessel containing jewelry and coins from the time of Valens, who ruled Egypt from A.D. 364 to 378, and a number of tombs continued to be cut into the sandstone even after that date. Unfortunately, most Egyptian citizens paid a price for the successes of the Roman Empire, which is said to have been an especially punitive government that exercised its control with a heavy hand.

Naphtali Lewis, one of the leading Greco-Roman scholars of the past half-century, has written: "The lot of the humble and the poor was not enviable anywhere in the Roman Empire . . . but the population of Egypt appears to have been singled out for exceptionally harsh treatment. Roman policy toward Egyptians conveys to us a quality of repression suggestive of vindictiveness." We know from the detailed census records kept during this time that the government imposed heavy taxes and strict punishment in debtors' prisons for those who could not pay. All males who were not citizens of Rome or of the autonomous Greek communities—in other words, Egyptians—paid a poll tax from the age of fourteen. Peasant labor and natural resources, such as grain, were more systematically exploited. Lewis reports that life expectancy decreased to the astonishing age of twenty-two-and-a-half to twenty-five years during the Roman occupation, a low point not experienced in the region since the agricultural communities of the Late Neolithic Period.

This increase in mortality could have been caused by a combination of high stress levels and low nutrition, as well as by confrontation with violent forces.

However, much of this information has been based on studies of Egyptians from the Nile Valley, and in spite of these conclusions, we still do not know much about the quality of life for the people of Egypt during Roman rule, especially in the oases, where fewer records were kept. Ancient Egyptian texts and stelae tell us that the oases were far enough away from the centralized government to be a possible place of refuge from Roman soldiers, and evidence from ancient papyri reveals, as Naphtali writes, that "the flight of peasants into the desert from the rich valley was not uncommon under Roman rule."

On the basis of census documents kept by the Romans in order to collect taxes more efficiently, we can estimate the ancient population of Egypt as a whole during the Roman Period at about seven million, but we cannot estimate the number of people who were living in Bahariya and its outlying areas at that time. Our lack of information about the oases is a result of the fact that ancient historians examined their societies from the top down. Since Egyptians were required to communicate with the Roman government in Greek, most Egyptians are not represented in the history of the Roman era. Written records on ostraca and papyrus tell us that Hadrian, one of ten Roman rulers during A.D. 213, oversaw the military forces at Bahariya. Although the post seems to have been well protected, the Libyan Nobatai people, who were settled on its borders, destroyed the villages there in A.D. 298. A map dated to the year 399 shows additional Roman and Byzantine military camps bordering Bahariya in several areas, including El Haiz, which we shall explore in later chapters.

Modern bioarchaeological evidence could serve to fill in some of the gaps left by written documentation, but conclusions drawn from X-ray studies of mummies are not always accurate because the exact dates of skeletal remains cannot be calculated, as tombs were used over long

**The Coptic church near the Roman settlement of El Haiz, built next to an ancient well**

periods of time and mummies were sometimes moved. The examples excavated from Bahariya's tombs, however, can be dated on the basis of architectural evidence and undisturbed artifacts found in the tombs, and, as we have seen, are now being studied with X rays and other techniques, including DNA studies. So far, the results suggest that people of the oases suffered less than Egyptians living in the Nile Valley, close to the center of government and military power.

There is significant evidence that Christianity existed in Bahariya during the Roman occupation. The Coptic saints Bartholomew and George are mentioned by the twelfth-century Armenian historian Abou Saleh as being connected with Bahariya, and a church in El Haiz established in Saint George's name is said to have contained his sacred remains. Other Coptic monuments can be found in El Qasr, El Bawiti, and Mandeesha, but the most important Christian relic in the Oasis is a church in El Haiz, which Fakhry described as dating to the end of the fifth century or the beginning of the sixth, and which may have been an even older place of Christian worship (see chapter 10). It is difficult to ascertain just how long Christianity was practiced by the people of Bahariya and exactly in what form. Fakhry believed, for example, that the settlement of El Haiz was not even inhabited during the Middle Ages, between the twelfth and seventeenth centuries.

The life and teachings of the prophet Mohammed had a profound effect on the people of Egypt after the seventh century A.D. One of the few references we have to the oases during this period is a report that Amir Ibn el-As, commander of the Arab army that conquered Egypt in 641, sent troops under Uqba Ibn-Nafea, overseer of the army, to insure political stability in the Western Desert. However, it is possible that remote oases outside the main centers of Bahariya did not adopt Islam until the sixteenth century, long after it was established as the official religion of Egypt.

During the Middle Ages, Bahariya continued to be a much-used trade route to other parts of northern Africa, and as a result, it maintained its political and economic importance even as the government of Egypt continued to change hands. However, the Oasis eventually stopped all production of wine after the laws of Allah banned the consumption of alcohol, which is still in effect, although wine production has continued for personal use, if not for trade. By the eighteenth century, thanks to Benoit de Maillet, French consul-general under Louis XIV, the European interest in ancient Egyptian antiquities began to increase until Napoleon himself took scientists and artists along with his soldiers in 1798 and produced the first comprehensive archaeological survey of the region. After becoming pasha of Egypt under the Ottoman Turks in 1805, Mohammed Ali, and his government and that of his successors made substantial efforts to link Bahariya more readily with the Nile Valley, specifically the region of El Menia and Asyut. Subsequently, numerous archaeologists, historians, adventurers, collectors, and tourists thronged to Egypt in search of artifacts and information, and several of them visited Bahariya and wrote about its monuments and their beauty.

The famous explorer and excavator Giovanni Belzoni, who was responsible for removing so many ancient artifacts from Egypt to the European market, mistakenly associated Bahariya with the oracle of Amun, which is actually located in Siwa Oasis. Because of this error, Belzoni made some of the earliest detailed descriptions of monuments in the oases. Later, in 1820, the archaeologist Gailliud recorded important information about some monuments that no longer exist, including the Roman victory arch at El Haiz. In 1825 the English archaeologist Sir John Gardner Wilkinson visited the palaces of El Zabu and El Maishra and a few of the buildings around El Qasr. An adventurer named Vershow claimed in 1876 to have visited rooms below ground containing pottery and coffins, perhaps the tombs in El Bawiti cut at the bottom of shafts we are only now exploring. Also in 1876, a German archaeologist, Ascherson, visited Bahariya, described a number of its monuments, and took some of its artifacts to Berlin.

On his way to visit Siwa Oasis and the Fayum, Georg Steindorff was the first to discover the tomb of Amenhotep Huy (see chapter 14). He also found, in front of some houses in El Qasr, an alabaster statue of the priest Zed-Khonsu-efankh, whose tomb we still hope to uncover. In 1903 Beadnell and Ball made the first thorough archaeological survey of most of the Western Desert sites and created an excellent reference book about its geological features, which we still use today. In 1908 an irrigation inspector for the French-Egyptian government entered brief descriptions of Oasis tombs into the *Annales de Service,* published by the Supreme Council of Antiquities in Egypt. And the Egyptian archaeologist Ahmed Fakhry made the most comprehensive recent contribution to the study of Bahariya monuments with publications describing in detail what he found there on extended visits during the 1930s and 1940s.

Traditions in the communities located in the oasis areas have always outlasted those in the more centralized areas along the Nile Valley, because the distance from urban culture tends, of course, to keep the oasis dwellers relatively insulated. Nowhere has this been more effectively documented than in the reports written by Ahmed Fakhry. Not surprisingly, however, rapid changes have occurred in the oasis towns and their residents during the last fifty years, since the introduction of improved roads, a railroad, and television.

Some things have changed, but since the list of what has stayed the same is shorter, I will begin with that. For example, the people who now live in Bahariya are considered, for the most

A farmer commutes on his donkey to collect food for his animals.

*Below:* A Bedouin trader from the desert outside Bahariya Oasis visits the market in El Bawiti.

part, to be the direct descendants of ancient Egyptian inhabitants mixed with the blood of Bedouins and some immigrants from Middle Egypt or the other oases who came to do business along the trade route. Merchants are still the richest people in Bahariya today, just as they were in ancient times, and agriculture remains the primary source of income for the Oasis, although dates rather than wine are its principal agricultural export. Interestingly, some traditions prevail from pharaonic times, even if in some cases they are no longer practiced for the same reason. For example, mourning the deceased entails putting water in vases on their graves and scattering grain around it. Moslems say they do it to attract birds to the site, but the same ancient Egyptian practice was based on the belief that the person's spirit, the *ba,* took the form of a bird with the head of the deceased and when it returned to visit its body, it required water and food for sustenance. Many local Egyptians still believe in the power of magic, although it is impossible to say to what extent. Some even practice spells today in order to induce specific effects, ranging from love to revenge.

The same artesian-well system has been employed since at least the Pharaonic Period, and in several cases, the ancient wells are still being used. One can see rope marks worn into the sandstone from thousands of years of pulling up heavy buckets of water. Unfortunately, however, most of the wells were abandoned years ago as the water table gradually lowered, making the essential ingredient for the maintenance of their culture—water—increasingly difficult to access. In fact, one of the major problems facing the people of Bahariya over the last half century has been the depletion of their water supply and the incessant encroachment of sand dunes, which are covering wells, gardens, farms, and even homes. Owing to a substantial loss of farmland, which reached a crisis point during the 1950s, thousands of long-established residents fled to the cities, mainly Cairo, to search for work in order to support their families. The population of Bahariya subsequently dropped as low as 6,000, but by 1986 the number of inhabitants increased to nearly 20,000 and today there are about 27,000 people living there. What has brought about this resurgence of life to the Oasis?

At the beginning of the twentieth century, Bahariya was part of the Minia and Fayum Governates and later the Mersa Matrouh Governate, but in 1972 the Oasis was finally placed under the official jurisdiction of the Giza Governate, which is why scientific excavations are now conducted under the auspices of the Giza Antiquities Department. Along with this change in government came an improved road system. Before 1973, there were only two ways to drive to Bahariya Oasis—the ancient camel route from Bahnasa and the equally ancient road from Cairo—and both were unpaved. One needed a four-wheel-drive vehicle to transport goods and people and even then the trip was very difficult, taking from three to ten days, almost the same amount of time it took to travel by camel. The nearest town in Farafra Oasis lay 115 miles beyond Bahariya, a full day's trip.

By the end of 1973, both of the old caravan routes had been paved, and nowadays anyone can easily drive a rented car from Cairo to Bahariya or take one of the regularly scheduled daily buses and sit back and watch a movie. Thanks to the increased number of visitors, the people of Bahariya have an active business bartering dates, along with olives, olive oil, apricots, grapes,

Date palms are still a dominating feature of the Oasis landscape, just as they were in ancient times.

**A farm in El Bawiti surrounded by a modern mud-brick wall**

watermelons, and citrus fruits in return for tea, sugar, soap, fabrics, seeds, and other items not indigenous to the Oasis, just as they did in ancient times. Unfortunately, however, agricultural and animal diseases were also imported along these improved routes; orange trees brought in from the Nile Valley carried infestations from fruit flies and introduced diseases that have afflicted the local melon and tomato crops. Imported cows transmitted liver disease to Oasis cattle, and this is now spreading to sheep, buffalo, and even camels. The recent use of pesticides in El Haiz is beginning to create reproductive problems and anatomical malformations in several species. On the other hand, health care for people and the overall standard of living have greatly improved. At one time the local barber was the one to whom the sick turned for treatment, but now each town has a clinic, and the central hospital is capable of handling minor surgery. Specialized doctors and dentists come every month from Cairo to attend to more complicated cases.

The Egyptian government created the Organization for Desert Development Projects in 1959, and many who had emigrated to other areas were successfully lured back to Bahariya to dig more wells and cultivate more land. As an odd result of bureaucratic regulations established at that time, however, anyone wishing to build a waterwheel in a certain area must first purchase that land, but no one can purchase land unless it is already cultivated, which requires a waterwheel.

In the mid-1970s, railroad tracks were laid down across the dunes as part of a government plan to exploit the iron-ore deposits that are so abundant in Bahariya Oasis. This project, of course, increased available jobs, so that residents are no longer as dependent on growing dates and other produce that require good soil. The mine in El Gedidah currently employs seven hundred workers and transports eight thousand tons of iron ore to Cairo every day. Another ambitious government-sponsored project to begin in the near future is the construction of a canal system designed to divert water from the lake in Aswan to the oases. Once this system is operational, it should alleviate the ongoing problems created as springs dry up. Electricity was also installed during the 1970s, modernizing the town of El Bawiti virtually overnight, and television inevitably followed, in 1986. By 1987 the Oasis had its own television station and became connected with the rest of Egypt.

One major change brought about by the easy access to Cairo, as well as by the introduction in 1952 of an Egyptian law requiring all children to attend school, is the dramatic increase in educational opportunities. At least 80 percent or more of the Oasis population is now literate. Most young people are educated through secondary school, and many even go on to university. The chance for residents to work in official government departments has diminished some of the pressures of a primarily agricultural economy, although at the same time, the diversification in jobs has led to increased social stratification and new tensions within the populace, as well as heightened competition for a limited number of jobs.

One can also point to the fact that before these modern amenities were introduced, especially television, Bahariya maintained its own heritage and traditions, but now modernization appears to have destroyed most of the local culture. For example, women and girls once proudly wore long, black, formless dresses embroidered with bright red, green, and yellow lines and silver coin-like decorations. A band of red linen would be wrapped around a black head covering or through

A poultry farmer weighing a sale at the open market in El Bawiti

Some villagers of El Bawiti outside a row of mud-brick dwellings

*Below:* Young women in Islamic dress coming home from school in El Bawiti

the hair, and nearly every part of the body was embellished with jewelry. Silver disks dangled over the forehead from a headband etched with plant forms, and most women wore a pair of large hoop earrings, often hung with silver disks, as well as silver bracelets and anklets, gold nose rings, and necklaces made of glass beads, amber, or large silver disks. Some even chose to decorate their foreheads and chins with tattoos. For evening wear, women would don big black cloaks over their finery. Women now dress as they do in Cairo, where attire consists of plain robes and head coverings, which at times are worn over the face. Some women may continue to wear traditional garments, but for the most part they no longer display their unique costume proudly, preferring to remain hidden indoors. Indeed, in all my visits to the town of El Bawiti, I have never met a woman or seen one walking in the streets, and though the local craftsmen continue to make traditional jewelry and scarves, they are primarily sold as novelty items to tourists. Interestingly, men often wear the traditional long, white *gallabia* with a short skirt over it and a white scarf on their heads, although many have adopted modern pants and shirts.

There is a new police station in El Bawiti. The government has also built a sports center in every small village, and El Bawiti, El Qasr, Mandeesha, El Zabu, El Agouz, El Kebala, El Hara, and El Haiz all have soccer and other sports teams that compete with each other. Unfortunately, as of 1999, the entire Oasis still had only one phone line, but a central telephone system is scheduled for installation in the year 2000 so that residents will be able to make international calls. And there is still no Oasis airport, although one is being constructed as I write, so that tourists, archaeologists, and local entrepreneurs will soon be able to fly to Bahariya from Cairo in less than an hour. There are hotels now, including the El Beshmo Lodge, where we stay, and the English House, a mansion originally inhabited by the Turks during the Ottoman Empire. Just two hours or so south by car is the intriguing White Desert, where rock outcroppings formed from calcium deposits create a unique environment. Experiencing this section of the desert is like going to the moon. Perhaps one day tourism will supplement the economy, as visitors come from all over the world to visit the Oasis sites.

One of the many natural hot springs overlooking the Oasis

*Below:* El Beshmo Lodge in El Bawiti, where the excavation team stays each season

# EGYPTIAN RELIGIOUS BELIEFS

ALTHOUGH THE STYLES AND METHODS OF MUMMIFICATION IN ANCIENT Egypt varied considerably from one dynastic period to the next, spiritual beliefs remained remarkably consistent for more than three thousand years. In spite of centuries of invading cultures, Egyptian mythology and ritual worship continued unabated. Even when Greece and Rome usurped leadership of the land, bringing with them highly developed cultures and their own array of deities, the foreign rulers often adopted the complex Egyptian pantheon of gods and religious practices. Only much later did the separate mythologies begin to merge, as the invaders chose to be Egyptianized rather than imposing their religion on those they now ruled, a powerful testament to the durability of ancient Egyptian culture. It was not until the advent of Christianity that the old religion gave way, and even then many of the images and basic beliefs of the newly formalized religion derived from the traditional Egyptian belief system. In fact, Roman Christians may have replicated some of the favorite Egyptian deities in order to exercise more power over their subjects. For example, the predominant mother figure, the goddess Isis, who is often depicted with her son Horus in her lap, may be the original version of the Virgin holding the Christ Child. The most significant contribution made by Egyptian mythology to Christianity, today's most widespread religion, was probably the belief in resurrection after death into eternal life, known to ancient Egyptians as the afterlife.

The main tenet of the Egyptian belief system was that rebirth always followed death. This was not just a symbolic notion but was based on the observation of nature. The ancients were firmly convinced of the never-ending cycles of life after death because they experienced the daily rising and setting of the sun and the renewal of the land through the yearly flooding of the Nile. The cyclical disappearance of certain stars during the month was also evidence that the god Osiris, though relegated to the underworld, still lived on in the night sky. It could only be expected, therefore, that their own bodies worked in the same way. Death, they observed, inevitably led to a new beginning.

However, several requirements had to be fulfilled and challenges faced before one could attain new life in eternity. Although death was not seen as an end, it was considered a dangerous journey fraught with threatening forces. The deceased had to navigate through labyrinths in the underworld, which required the use of maps and the repeating of secret incantations, or spells, at every stage along the way. All of the necessary information, including answers to questions asked by the gods, was written in a kind of guide to the underworld, a collection of funerary texts called *The Spells for Coming Forth by Day*, later known as *The Book of the Dead*. This collection of spells—first inscribed on pyramid walls, then on coffins and papyrus manuscripts, and eventually, later in the

A clay statue, found in one of the tombs in the Valley of the Golden Mummies, of the motherhood goddess Isis holding her son, Horus, in a pose similar to that of the Virgin and Child in later Christian imagery.

*Below:* A gold bracelet decorated wit the *wedjat* eye

*Page 120:* Osiris, king of the underworld, sitting on his throne wearing his crown and holding scepters as painted in Nefertari's Nineteenth Dynasty tomb at the Valley of the Queens, Luxor

Late and Ptolemaic Periods, directly on the mummies' linen and cartonnage—had to be interred with the deceased for use on the journey.

Protective amulets made of gold, stone, or faience, a brightly colored glasslike material, also accompanied the body on its way to the underworld. The amulets ranged from images of the gods to scarabs and *wedjat* eyes (the eye of the god Horus), each with its own powers against specific evils. Amulets were sometimes wrapped by the hundreds inside royal mummies, while nonroyal mummies brought with them only a few necklaces, rings, or bracelets. By the Late and Greco-Roman Periods, however, gold amulets were used by anyone who could afford them.

The final goal of the journey was the Hall of Judgment, where the deceased would meet

Red granite sarcophagus of King Thutmose III in his burial chamber at the Valley of the Kings, Luxor

*Below left:* The deceased and his wife worship Osiris on his throne in this papyrus of the New Kingdom.

*Below:* An excerpt from *The Book of the Dead* inscribed in the burial chamber of Thutmose III

Anubis, the jackal-headed god of embalming, and Thoth, the god of wisdom, who would introduce the deceased to Osiris, god of the dead and ruler of the underworld. The heart of the deceased, considered the organ of both intelligence and emotion, would be placed on a scale to be weighed against the feather of Maat, the goddess of truth and justice. The deceased would then recite a series of negative confessions like the following to a tribunal of judges:

O Dark One, who came forth from darkness, I have not cursed.

O He Who Brings His Offering, who came forth from Asyut, I have not been violent.

O Proclaimer of Voice, who came forth from Unas, I have not confounded truth.

This ritual constituted a time of reckoning for one's behavior throughout the previous life, an

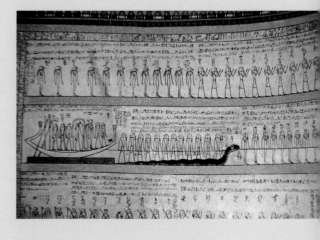

opportunity for the deceased to proclaim before the tribunal that he had never (among other things) stolen, killed, been sullen, loud, or hot-tempered, committed adultery, slain sacred cattle, brought any lawsuits, or disputed the king. The strict code of ethics outlined in *The Book of the Dead* gives us some idea of what the ancients regarded as socially acceptable behavior, although it does not necessarily tell us what their actual behavior was, since every individual was apparently assured of passing the test. This journey of the deceased, from mummification to the underworld, was based on the original myth of Osiris, ruling god of Egypt, who was murdered by his brother Seth, mummified, buried, and then resurrected into the afterlife. Osiris's story all but guaranteed that everyone else would follow the same fate by passing through the Hall of Judgment successfully and being granted eternal life.

The ancients believed that each individual had several aspects. The physical aspect was considered the weakest because it was susceptible to death and deterioration. A person's *ka* was a kind of spiritual body double, while the *ba*, represented by the shape of a bird with the face of the deceased hovering above his body, was like our concept of a human soul. These could live forever so long as they had a body to return to, but if an individual allowed his body to deteriorate, it was believed he would lose all hope for eternity and his *ka*, having no vein through which to flow, would be doomed to search forever for a body that no longer existed.

*Above and opposite:* **Osiris presides over the Hall of Judgment in the Twenty-sixth Dynasty tomb of Bannantiu in Bahariya Oasis, with Hathor behind him and the monster Amem ready to devour the body of the deceased if his heart outweighs the feather of Maat.**

To avoid this fate, embalmed bodies, or mummies, were interred with a statue of the deceased that the *ka* and *ba* could recognize and that could take the place of the body in case it deteriorated beyond recognition. Should the replica also be destroyed, the *ka* or *ba* could live on in the person's name, or *ren*, which was also left behind in the tomb, often in the form of inscriptions on commemorative stelae, or stone slabs that were mounted on walls or in niches (called false doors). It was the responsibility of the deceased's heir to give offerings and insure that his parent's name became eternal. After the ultimate reunion of the deceased's *ka* and *ba*, he would finally achieve the state of being a transfigured spirit or shadow, known as an *akh*.

If the body were properly preserved, through the mummification process known as *khet*, and the scales of Maat were balanced, the traveler through the underworld would be allowed to reach his destination as an *akh*, become young again, and live forever in Iaru, or paradise. The Egyptians' literal conception of Iaru is not completely understood, although in certain texts it is referred to as living among the stars. In any event, Iaru was a world similar to the one people lived in on earth, which is why the deceased needed food for the journey, furniture, favorite games, and, of course, the body. The Egyptians therefore began to develop ways of preserving the physical body in order that the deceased could live in peace in the afterlife and benefit from the offerings left in the tomb (see chapter 9 for more on mummification practices).

For three hundred years before the birth of Christ, the Greeks ruled Egypt under the Ptolemaic Dynasty, named for Ptolemy I, general to Alexander the Great. In 30 B.C. the country was absorbed into the Roman Empire, and eventually virtually all traces of Egyptian religion and mythology disappeared. This seems to have been, for the most part, a gradual process over nearly a millennium, but it represents a major transition that we seek to understand through the study of Greco-Roman settlements such as those at Bahariya.

In spite of the existence of separate religions in Egypt at the time of Alexander's conquest, the most prevalent belief system was that of the ancient Egyptians, with only slight stylistic

The goddess Maat protects the name of Nefertari in her cartouche within her tomb.

*Opposite top:* Bannantiu is led by the goddess Maat to the scales, where his heart will be weighed against the feather of truth to determine if he can proceed to spend eternity in Iaru, the ancient Egyptian version of paradise.

*Opposite bottom:* Detail from the chest plate of one of the gold Greco-Roman mummies showing one of the four sons of Horus, a traditional Egyptian god, holding up a knife to protect the deceased against evil

variations in the depiction of the gods. The Greeks, whose language was the official language of Egypt after Alexander's conquest, gave the name Osiris to the principal Egyptian god Usir, and they called Hap, the sacred bull, by the Greek name Apis. By Roman times these two gods had merged as Osorapis, eventually Serapis, whose place of worship became the Serapeum at Alexandria. Thoth, god of the moon as well as wisdom, who is often depicted weighing the heart of the deceased in the Hall of Judgment, was identified by the Greeks with their own Hermes, who led the souls of the people. Bes, god of pleasure, who protected pregnant women and children, later took on a role as protector of the deceased and was associated with Dionysos and later Bacchus. Hathor, goddess of beauty and love, became the female manifestation of Osiris and was associated with death and rebirth, as well as with her Greek counterpart, Aphrodite. The *ka* and *ba* were eventually combined in the concept of the human soul. It was not until after the second century A.D., however, that Egypt witnessed more radical changes in religious beliefs and in the way Egyptians thought about life after death.

Elaborate preparation and burial of the deceased were costly measures that only the royal family and members of the nobility could afford in ancient times. An expensive funeral procession was the only way to keep evil spirits at bay and to insure an easy life after death. The most significant change that took place during Roman rule was that the most expensive funerary rituals and magical incantations were eventually discarded, with the consequence that every individual could now be promised a place in eternity regardless of wealth or status.

We understand this from the following story told by the High Priest Khaemwase, who

claimed to have traversed the underworld through the Cemetery of Memphis. His tale, or parable, informs us of the shift in values taking place during the Greco-Roman Period. He recounts witnessing two funerals in the underworld, one of them for a wealthy man behind whom stood women weeping and running after him to the burial place and hordes of followers in richly decorated uniforms. The second funeral was for a poor man, who was given a tomb covered with mats. No mourning women or richly dressed companions were present at his funeral because he could not afford them. In fact, no one came to the poor man's funeral.

When Khaemwase arrived at the sixth stage of the underworld, he saw both men being judged before Osiris seated on his golden chair. Beside Osiris stood Anubis and Thoth, presiding gods in the Hall of Judgment, and in front of him was the scale of justice. Near the scale was the hippopotamus-goddess, Taweret, ready to devour the deceased if his heart should prove to be heavier than the feather of Maat. The high priest found that the rich man, who had been given an extravagant funeral, had not done one good thing in the course of his fortunate life that would give him happiness in the next. But the poor man passed through the Hall of Judgment into life everlasting because his heart was pure, weightless as the feather.

By Roman times an individual's good behavior in daily life became the sole criterion for reaching Iaru. Whether the deceased were rich or poor, no amount of spells, amulets, mourners, maps, or magic could help. Although Osiris still presided with his gods, the many gateways of the underworld were reduced to the single concept of a judgment before the gates of heaven—a concept that may have carried over into Christian doctrine. Not even the funerary figures, or *shabtis*, designed to spare the deceased from menial labor in the afterlife, could help the deceased pass successfully through this gate to eternal life if he had done nothing helpful or kind during his lifetime. Egyptians gradually discarded this magical belief and replaced it with the idea that all the good things enjoyed by the rich man who had done little good in his life would be taken from him and given to the poor man who had lived a good life.

Maat, goddess of truth and justice, spreads her wings over the entrance to the New Kingdom tomb of Queen Nefertari. Figures of Anubis, the jackal-god, sit on either side to protect the deceased.

Below: The four sons of Horus stand before Osiris on his throne in the center panel of the tomb painting below. Gods and goddesses protect and assist the deceased in various ways on their journey through the underworld.

We cannot neglect the evidence that the majority of ancient Egyptians, especially the destitute laborers, probably suffered a great deal under Roman rule, but this new belief must have granted some peace of mind to those who no longer had to concern themselves with the expense of a funeral. Before transcendence could take place, however, one was still required to preserve one's physical body according to the techniques developed centuries earlier that had become the art and science of Egyptian mummification.

# A HISTORY
# OF MUMMIFICATION

The ancient Egyptians developed remarkably sophisticated medical treatments for disease using both surgery and natural remedies. They understood the properties and consequent effects of mixing several substances together, and some of these formulas have been passed down to us through surviving medical papyri. Considering their applied knowledge of medicine and anatomy, along with their need to prepare themselves for the afterlife, it is not surprising that the early Egyptians devised a highly effective method of physically preserving their dead. Mummification is a unique combination of medicine and magic, and we have only gradually come to terms with the vast amount of information available about its methods, tools, and materials. As for the ancient rituals and spells associated with mummification, we have much still to learn.

TRADITIONAL MUMMIFICATION PRACTICES  More than five thousand years ago, the ancient inhabitants of Egypt simply covered the dead with animal skins or linen and buried them, wrapped in mats or enclosed in egg-shaped pots, at the bottom of holes dug near the edge of agricultural lands. Perhaps it was when they realized that the dry desert sand helped to preserve the skeleton and keep skin on the bones that they began to investigate methods to augment this dehydration process. The earliest stage in the development of mummification began in Predynastic Egypt, when Egyptians used various substances to seal the flesh and wrapped the body of the dead very tightly with linen. Human remains found at El Kab in Upper Egypt show traces of oil and other materials that had been added to the body of the deceased.

Some of the earliest evidence of royal mummification dates to the First and Second Dynasties, about 3000 B.C. Parts of a human arm decorated with bracelets composed of amulets made of gold and semiprecious stones were found in the tomb of King Djer at Abydos. Some scholars believe that the arm may have been that of a queen or a high-ranking official connected with Djer, although it may have belonged to the king himself. Skeletal remains were also discovered inside the Step Pyramid in Saqqara and may be those of King Djoser. Remains of Sneferu, the first pharaoh of the Fourth Dynasty, were discovered with resin inside the empty skull, which tells us that by this time Egyptians had begun to solve the problem of deterioration by applying resin to preserve the inner cavities from which the brain and other internal organs—the first parts of the body to deteriorate—had been removed. Third Dynasty burials found at Meidum in Middle Egypt indicate that organic material was placed in containers after removal and given a special place within the tomb. Dried organic material still remains in the bottom of an alabaster box found east of the Great Pyramid in the tomb of Queen Hetepheres, the mother of Khufu. This box was an early version of what would later became known as canopic jars, in which organs were preserved separately from the wrapped mummy.

The wooden inlaid anthropoid coffin of Queen Meryt-Amun, a style used especially during the New Kingdom. (Egyptian Museum, Cairo)

*Below:* The almost perfectly preserved features of the New Kingdom mummy of Ramses II (Egyptian Museum, Cairo) demonstrate the highly sophisticated mummification techniques developed by the ancient Egyptians.

*Opposite:* The sun-god Ra as a mummy, and protected by Isis and Nephtys, ready to be united with Osiris, in a wall painting in Nefertari's tomb in the Valley of the Queens, Luxor

*Page 130:* The four canopic jars of the Twenty-sixth Dynasty tomb of Iuf-aa found in Abusir. The jars were intended to hold the kidneys, liver, stomach, and lungs of the deceased.

Wooden coffins and stone sarcophagi began to appear in burials of the Early Dynastic Period (3100–2686 B.C.). By the end of the Old Kingdom (2686–2181 B.C.), linen bandages were stiffened with plaster, or gesso, to create a case for the corpse known as a cartonnage mummy before it was put in the coffin. Often this material was applied only to the head and sides of the body and modeled to appear more lifelike. By the Middle Kingdom, mummies were decorated with paint and gilding. By the Seventeenth Dynasty, c. 1600 B.C., anthropoid coffins were shaped like human forms, to which elaborate masks were later added.

The New Kingdom (1550–1069 B.C.) is the period in which the art of mummification reached its peak. We are fortunate to have the impressive tomb of Tutankhamun, which proves just

The four alabaster canopic jars of the New Kingdom pharaoh Tutankhamun with his head depicted on each lid (Egyptian Museum, Cairo)

how elaborate interment had become by the Eighteenth Dynasty. After the body of this relatively minor young king had been wrapped in sixteen layers of linen, it was placed inside a gold anthropoid coffin, which was then enclosed in two more boxes and sealed inside a limestone sarcophagus.

By the Late Period (747–332 B.C.), when Egypt was ruled by a series of foreign rulers, the process of mummification gradually lost its purpose, and methods changed. Preparation was not as carefully managed, and bodies were now often eviscerated through anal enemas rather than through incisions. The liberal use of resin seems to have replaced the more time-consuming processes of dehydration and anointing, and bodies were no longer placed along a north-south axis, as had always been the case in the past.

In Predynastic burials the deceased's hands were placed over the face, and the body was usually left lying on its side facing the rising sun in the east. By the time of the Old Kingdom, mummies were placed on their backs with their arms generally held along their sides. In various periods, the hands of some mummies were made to cover their genitals, but it was not until the New Kingdom and then again in Roman burials centuries later that mummies had their hands crossed over the chest in the familiar Osirian position.

A rich source of information about the materials and tools of mummification came from the discovery of caches buried near various tombs in which embalmers had discarded leftover

In the Twenty-sixth Dynasty tomb of Bannantiu in Bahariya Oasis, Anubis is shown mummifying the deceased, flanked by the mourning goddesses Isis and Nephtys.

material when their job was completed. Tools found in these caches include incision knives, tweezers, hooks for the nose, and enemas, along with embalming tables, most often made of wood with the four legs carved in the shape of lions' heads. Traces of preserving materials, including a form of salt called natron, as well as oil and charcoal, were also left behind by embalmers in the tomb of royal mummies discovered in Deir el-Bahri in 1881.

The most important depiction of mummification found in any tomb is a wall painting found in a burial at Thebes dating to the Nineteenth Dynasty of the New Kingdom. The chamber of the tomb illustrates the different stages of the operation, including two scenes that show the anointing with oils. In another Theban tomb appear carved scenes of a mummy being wrapped and anointed, followed by images depicting the preparation of the face mask with cartonnage. A man is shown putting his hand inside a large pottery vessel that may have been used for storing mummification materials.

The word "mummy" seems to have evolved from the false belief that Persian bitumen, or *mummia,* was the substance used to embalm ancient cadavers, but we now know that the resin used was made from tree sap. Other materials, such as beeswax, were described by the Roman historian Pliny, and DNA testing later confirmed the use of beeswax to seal orifices, eyes, and linen wrapping. But the most important material for the drying process was natron, a natural salt that had

On another wall in the tomb of Bannantiu, Anubis is shown mummifying the deceased, while Isis and Nephtys stand on either side mourning his passage. Beneath the enbalming table are Bannantiu's canopic jars. In the image below, the mummy of Bannantiu stands between Isis and Nephtys.

accumulated along the shores and beds of ancient lakes in Wadi Natrun in Lower Egypt, El Kab in Upper Egypt, and outside the Fayum Oasis.

The methods of ancient mummification were described in detail by Herodotus, the Greek "father of history," who visited Egypt about 450 B.C. He wrote about three methods of preserving the dead, each of which took seventy days. The most expensive involved the extraction of the brain through the nostrils with a hook and the removal of the internal organs through an incision in the flank. The inner cavity was then washed with palm wine and spices, sewn up again, and covered with natron. After the drying process, which took forty days, the prepared cadaver was wrapped in linen and placed in a coffin. In the second method, the viscera were removed by anal enema, but the body was still treated with natron and oils. The least expensive method of mummification was simply to administer the enema, dry the corpse and wrap it, and then return it to the relatives of the deceased.

A later historian, Diodorus of Sicily (active c. 40 B.C.) also attempted to explain this practice, which was unique to Egypt at the time, and his observations have since been confirmed by modern studies. He noted that the viscera were cleaned with incense, and that after the inner cavity was coated with resin, the outside was massaged with oils. In the New Kingdom, mummy interiors were packed with linen or sawdust, and the nose was sometimes propped up with a bone to make the mummy look more lifelike. To insure that the fingernails did not fall off, the skin on the fingers was cut and then tied around the nails, although an extravagant later process achieved the same goal by fitting each finger with a gold tip. One aspect of mummification that remained relatively consistent throughout ancient history was that, while the heart was replaced inside the body, the brain, which was considered relatively useless for eternity, was discarded. Only lower-class mummies, for which the process of draining the brains would have been too expensive, are found with the brains intact.

The use of canopic jars to hold the organs necessary for the journey to the underworld appeared in the Old Kingdom. By the Middle Kingdom the jar lids were carved in the shape of human heads representing the deceased, so that the *ba* could recognize its own body parts. During the New Kingdom these containers of stone, wood, or pottery depicted the four sons of the god Horus, who were regarded as guardians of the internal organs.

In spite of the many books written about mummies and the evolving methods of preserving the dead, very few sources reveal the sacred rituals that accompanied the process of mummification. It is certain that bodies were systematically sanctified and that the embalming was imbued with symbolic significance. Embalmers were priests of the highest order, and mummification was one of the most important and most highly developed rituals known to the priesthood. Yet these secrets have been shrouded in mystery, and so mummification continues to intrigue scientists and laymen alike.

Diodorus wrote that the people who made the incisions were not well liked because they violated the bodies of the dead, and that they hid after finishing their job, so people would not stone them. But we now know that these were well-respected priests who played the role of gods during this process. They are often shown wearing the masks of gods such as Anubis, with two holes for the eyes. The priests performed their ritualistic work inside the *per ankh*, or purification place, and ceremoniously transported the body to the *per-nefer*, or beautiful temple. I have found signs of the existence of these temporary embalming workshops outside the tombs of Nefer and the priest Kai at Giza.

Underground mud-brick chambers of the royal tombs of the First and Second Dynasties in Abydos are the earliest form of royal cemeteries. Mastabas, or benchlike tombs, so named by the nineteenth-century French archaeologist Auguste Mariette after benches on which farmers sat,

Anubis, lord of the cemetery and god of embalming, sits on a pedestal in the tomb of Nefertari in the Valley of the Queens.

*Below:* Anubis is depicted here as a jackal-headed god, with the body of a man, protecting Nefertari. The priests who performed the seventy-day sacred ritual of embalming and wrapping the mummy are believed to have worn jackal masks.

constitute the next phase of burial for kings, nobility, and high officials. This aboveground burial was soon followed by the construction of pyramids, culminating in Khufu's Great Pyramid at Giza. The use of pyramidal structures over a burial structure recurred intermittently thereafter but never as impressively as during the Fourth Dynasty. For the most part, pyramids were not decorated with inscriptions until Unas of the Fifth Dynasty had *The Pyramid Texts,* the earliest version of the *Book of the Dead,* written on the walls of his tomb. In general, during the Old and Middle Kingdoms private tombs became increasingly complex chapels with several burial shafts inside. New Kingdom tombs, which were primarily located on the West Bank of Thebes, were shafts or ramps leading to underground chambers. The number of subterranean chambers ranges from three, as in the case of King Tutankhamun, to more than one hundred cut into the rock with astounding precision, as in the case of the newly excavated tomb of the sons of Ramses II in the Valley of the Kings.

Lower-class Egyptians often reused tombs constructed in earlier centuries or were buried in underground mud-brick complexes near the tombs of the rulers they served. The Tombs of the Pyramid Builders at Giza are a good example of this. Private tombs could also be niches cut in hills, shafts in solid rock, or even natural caves. Nonroyal individuals were not buried in expensive masks, decorated coffins, or elaborate sarcophagi but were laid instead on a thin layer of wood. In earlier stages, mummies were either buried alone or with a few family members. By the Third Intermediate Period, approximately five hundred years before the burials of the Greco-Roman Period, large numbers of coffins were interred together in one tomb.

## GRECO-ROMAN MUMMIFICATION

Greco-Roman cemeteries have been found throughout Egypt from Marina el-Alamein in the northwest to Nubia in the south. The most famous are the catacombs in Alexander the Great's capital city of Alexandria, but others have been found at Akhmim, Saqqara, Tuna el-Gebel, Kom Abu-Bellou, Aswan, and, most recently, Bahariya Oasis.

Mummification, once reserved for those of noble rank, was, by the end of the Late Period, offered to anyone who could afford it. This meant that every individual could be promised a place in eternity regardless of wealth or status, which may explain why there is such a range of mummy styles in Greco-Roman cemeteries. Each type of mummification represents a class within the culture, a factor that may have led to the loss of the funerary rituals and magic that were an integral part of ancient mummification practices. As the commercial aspect of mummification increased, an understanding of its sacred purpose gradually disappeared.

The mummies prepared by Greek and Roman embalmers do not reflect the same meticulous care taken by the ancient Egyptians. Specialists working in groups seem to have been in charge of separate tasks; priests no longer conducted the entire operation. Bodies were emptied, if they were emptied at all, through the use of enemas and were then filled with resin to the point of overflowing. (In later times, molten resin was simply slathered over the outside of the corpse.) Fewer layers of linen provided less protection before the body was returned to the family, and there are only a few examples of canopic jars interred with the body for use in the afterlife, demonstrating an erosion of the fundamental symbolic meaning intrinsic to ancient burials. Embalmers continued to remove the brain through the nose until the end of the second century A.D., but by the third and fourth centuries only a few cases are known in which the brain and viscera were

A painted scene from the tomb of Queen Nefertari shows her being protected by the goddesses Isis and Nephtys, who appear in the form of falcons.

removed. At this time organic material was left in the body; the arms were either crossed Osirian-style over the chest or placed on either side of the body.

Although preservation techniques were greatly simplified during the Late Period and especially after the Ptolemaic Period, the outer casings became distinctly varied and ornate. Linen wrapping became more sophisticated in the Ptolemaic Period and then reached its peak in Roman times. Wrappings were crisscrossed in a uniquely intricate pattern and sometimes decorated with gold. A new development in the first century A.D. was the wrapping of mummies in red-dyed linen. We found several mummies at Bahariya with traces of the red dye still present in their wrappings.

Extravagantly decorated cartonnage cases and masks were molded over the body and painted as they had been in the Twenty-first Dynasty. Facial features were represented realistically with the ears and head covered by a wig that extended over the shoulders and chest. For the first time in Egypt, women's breasts were painted on the outside of their mummies or articulated on breast plates. Commonly featured on the masks were religious scenes, patterned lines, and gods such as Anubis, Horus, Isis, Osiris, Nephtys, Maat, Thoth, and the four sons of Horus—a fascinating mix of Egyptian mythological beings painted in Hellenistic style. Greco-Roman mummies saw a resurgence in the use of gold coverings over faces, erections, breasts, and fingertips, as in the New Kingdom, and occasionally the entire body was gilded. Of course, gilding and cartonnage casing must not have been cheap; I estimate that during Roman rule, one mummy would have cost the equivalent of a family's income for one year.

As the embalmer became more merchant than priest, the Roman government placed increasingly heavy taxes on the wrapping and moving of mummies. The only aspect of this trade that

**The four sons of Horus, customarily depicted on tomb walls in Egypt (here from the tomb of Nefertari) to protect the deceased, were in Greco-Roman times painted directly on the cartonnage mummies.**

Gilded and cartonnage mummies found in the Greco-Roman cemetery at the Valley of the Golden Mummies

was not taxed was the transportation of the mummy across the Nile for burial. Families contracted with business enterprises to conduct the funeral service, including professional mourners who were paid to follow the dead to their graves, weeping. Embalmers during this period of commercialization were even known to have hired subcontractors and made money on work they no longer performed themselves.

The last of the stone sarcophagi were found in Ptolemaic cemeteries, such as those in Alexandria; the use of anthropoid coffins made a brief comeback before being discontinued in Roman times. Coffins at this time, if they were used at all, were usually made of wood and decorated inside with Egyptian motifs. Beginning in the first century A.D., a realistic portrait of the deceased was painted on a plaster mask, within which the head of the deceased was propped up so that it appeared to be waking up. The best known of these Roman-era funerary portraits, which represent the final development of the ancient Egyptian mask, were first found in the Fayum southwest of Cairo, hence the term "Fayum portrait," which applies to all depictions of this type. These exceptionally realistic family portraits were painted on wooden slabs or thick plaster that was often curved, vaulted, or round. The colors were made of natural minerals and the roots of plants, mixed with liquid wax and eggs. Similar portraits have been found in sites at Saqqara, Akhmim, Sheikh

*Shabtis* made of faïence found in the tomb of Iuf-aa. These funerary statuettes were interred with mummies, ideally one for each day of the year, to work on behalf of the deceased in the afterlife.

Abada in Middle Egypt, and Aswan. Archaeologists believe this style of mummification first appeared at the beginning or middle of the first century A.D. and disappeared at the beginning of the fourth.

I have been asked by several people how the golden mummies compare to the extraordinary painted portrait cases also dating to the Roman Period that were found at the Fayum at the beginning of the twentieth century. Although many mummies were found at that site, the architectural features of the tombs and the ways in which the mummies were prepared were completely different from those at Bahariya, perhaps because the Fayum was much closer to the Nile Valley and because most of the tombs were Christian burials.

Most of the information we have about the specific spells and incantations used by embalmers of this period come from papyri found in tombs dating from the turn of the first century A.D. The famous Rhind Papyrus, among others, describes some of the rituals connected with mummification and the necessary incantations recited during the wrapping of each part of the body. Apparently, at the time the papyri were written, there were seventeen rituals involved, a sacred number in ancient Egypt representing each of the seven orifices of the head, two legs, two arms, the front and back, and four internal organs. Each part was needed for the deceased to complete his treacherous journey to Iaru, so they had to be protected with magic spells as well as preserved. For thirty-six days, according to the Rhind Papyrus, the body was bathed in the Pool of Khonsu, named for a god of the moon, who was one of the most honored deities, and then it was laid to rest in the Place of Cleansing, a pool or vat filled with natron. The head was anointed with frankincense while the body received a mixture of other sacred oils before it was wrapped, each bandage having a magical name. The Turin Papyrus specifies which part of the body had to be wrapped first.

Although Herodotus had observed that the mummification process took seventy days, it seems that the entire operation could take less time if certain rituals were not performed. Therefore, we can assume that the Greeks and Romans included mummification rituals in some form, even if they were less exacting versions of the ancients' practices. One of the ancient rituals that was preserved well into the Greco-Roman Period was known as the Opening of the Mouth ceremony, which took place just before interment when the heir or a priest, holding a magical staff, would say to the deceased: "Open your nose so you can breathe. Open your eyes so you can see. Open your mouth so you can eat." The use of mummy portraits, for example, could have been loosely based on the ancient Egyptian belief in the resurrection and afterlife, a vestige of the idea that the mummy had to be recognizable in order for the *ba* to find and reunite with its physical body. Egyptians of the Roman Period no longer included *shabtis,* or statues of the deceased, to serve as their doubles, and they rarely even inscribed names in their tombs, the two other ancient methods used to orient the *ba.*

In fact, most Greco-Roman tombs lack inscriptions to tell us the names of those buried there, perhaps because few people other than priests could understand hieratic, the ancient script of Egypt. Egyptians in the Roman era therefore developed a new method to identify their deceased: they tied to each coffin a small wood tag with a brief Greek inscription giving the name of the deceased, the age and date at death, the name of the parents, and perhaps the date of the burial.

Since mummies were periodically taken in groups to be buried, this may have been the only way to determine which mummy belonged in which group tomb. The identity and status of certain individuals can be determined by specific markings. The Priest of the Sun, for example, is recognizable by seven beads of gold on the forehead representing a crown, whereas soldiers are distinguished by a leather belt painted in gold and silver around the coffin. The priests of Isis wore wide, decorated belts and large knots on their chests, and the priests of Serapis were identified by crowns with seven-sided stars.

One of the most significant changes in funerary ritual made during the Roman Period was that mummies were not moved directly to the tomb but were propped up in the house within their coffins for an indefinite length of time so the deceased could remain with its family and be remembered. During feasts and on special occasions, the mummy was even paraded before guests to remind them of their own mortality. Not surprisingly, these mummies were found in poor condition by having been left unattended and moved around like furniture or by having stood upright for long periods.

Funerary practices had also become very lax by this time. Groups of bodies were collected periodically from the homes where they had been displayed and delivered to cemeteries, where they were placed in mass burial pits. No longer was there any religious significance attached to

**Pictured in the Eighteenth Dynasty tomb of Tutankhamun at Luxor is King Ay, Tutankhamun's successor, performing the Opening of the Mouth ceremony on the young king, a rite every mummy had to undergo to insure that it could live, breathe, see, and eat in the afterlife.**

**The mummies found in the Valley of the Golden Mummies were placed in various positions rather than facing east, as in ancient Egyptian burials.**

their positioning, as there had been when the ancients consistently placed their dead facing east. Roman-era mummies were even occasionally stashed together in a single coffin, with the lid closed by force, crushing the plaster casts and skulls in the process. Group tombs were not only overcrowded but, as in much of Bahariya, bodies were also piled on top of each other without protective coffins. All of these factors, along with inefficient embalming techniques, explain why Roman mummies are often so badly damaged, while far older mummies maintain uncannily life-like expressions and positions.

This shabby treatment of the dead could have arisen from the lack of available grave space, although this is unlikely, since at Bahariya, where we found forty-three mummies in one tomb, the desert stretches out endlessly around the burial ground. It is more likely that the transformation of religious beliefs was already taking effect. In any case, the fact that burials had become so care-less indicates that much of the process had become devoid of its original intention, which was to preserve the physical body to live again forever in the land of Iaru.

We know that tombs during the Ptolemaic Period were built in imitation of the tombs of the Third Intermediate and the Late Periods. Some were constructed like temples, such as the tomb of Petosiris at Tuna el-Gebel in Middle Egypt, whose painted interiors represent a hybrid of Egyptian and Greek styles. The structure of another tomb at the same site resembles that of a house with doors and windows. There were three types of tombs used in the Roman Period: a single cylindrical shaft, which was commonly used for the general public; a rectangular shaft cut in the rock with tunnels or rooms off to the side usually containing families; and a staircase leading to a main burial chamber full of niches cut into a wall like benches, similar to those tombs seen in Rome and Kom el-Shugafa. We find all three types in Bahariya.

The knowledge of the ancients, applied in such practices as mummification and surgery, declined rapidly as the influx of Romans continued unabated, especially after the rise of formalized Christianity. The widely held belief in the afterlife, which necessitated mummification, continued for another two centuries after the birth of Christ, until the spread of the new religious doctrine of Christianity forbade what were considered pagan practices. For example, early Christians felt that too much emphasis was being placed on the physical body to the neglect of the spiritual in everyday life. By the Coptic Period, in fact, Saint Anthony, an Egyptian hermit who became the foremost symbol of early Christian monasticism, specifically insisted that his followers promise not to have him mummified. Extremely rare examples of mummies dating as late as the fourth to sixth century A.D. have been found, although the bodies had been dried with food salt rather than natron and the viscera were left inside the body to deteriorate. The mummies were covered with material other than linen, which had been considered sacred by the ancients, and they were buried in personal rather than ceremonial clothing. By the end of the sixth century, the practice of mummification had completely vanished from Egypt.

With the beginning of the Islamic era, Egyptians once again buried their dead in a fashion similar to that of the Predynastic Period, because Muslim practice is to beautify and wrap the body with white material, after which the body is laid in a hole in the dry desert and covered with sand and a large stone. But no other culture has ever matched the complex belief system, magic, and art of mummification of the ancient Egyptians.

**Archaeologist Tarek el-Awady examines the newly uncovered mummies in Tomb 62.**

# PART III
# EXCAVATIONS IN BAHARIYA OASIS

# THE ROMAN
# SETTLEMENT OF EL HAIZ

WHEN IN 1940 THE ARCHAEOLOGIST AHMED FAKHRY BEGAN TO CONDUCT a cursory excavation of the ancient settlement known as El Haiz, he found a few artifacts, including cases and beads from the Greco-Roman Period, fragments of pottery, and one empty wooden coffin. The only other interesting object was a small pendant of Anubis, which Fakhry deduced was from either the New Kingdom or the Ptolemaic Period. Based on the scant evidence he gathered from this discovery, he concluded: "Undoubtedly, the larger oasis fifty kilometers north of El Haiz was also thriving during the New Kingdom and will reap much new information about this time in our history."

As we have seen, Fakry was correct in his estimation. The area around El Bawiti to which he referred was for centuries a crucial caravan station for Bedouins, traders, merchants, and soldiers, as well as for foreign settlers who lived between Bahariya and Farafra Oasis to the southwest. Bahariya served as a crossroads for various cultures, and, as a result, the site now represents a cross section of the different types of people who passed through or settled there and left their unique marks and monuments behind. It is literally a gold mine of information about religions and social customs from ancient times to the Christian era.

What Fakhry did not imagine was the scope of information that the settlement of El Haiz itself would eventually offer. Nearly thirty miles southwest of El Bawiti, El Haiz would have had the same customs and ethnic makeup as its neighbor in Greco-Roman times, when the settlement benefited from four major water sources around which ancient life flourished from the second through the sixth century A.D. Fakhry estimated that there were fewer people living around each spring in the 1940s than there were in ancient times, in part because the lowering of the water table resulted in the abandonment of most ancient wells. There is substantially less vegetation now, making it necessary for villagers to travel much farther to obtain any variety of fruits, vegetables, and grains.

Currently El Haiz has no telephone line and only one large generator, which provides limited electricity during the day; it is shut off after 10:00 P.M. The road to El Haiz was paved in 1982, making it possible for the villagers to go by car rather than camel, donkey, or horse to trade their produce in El Bawiti, but the pavement, a mixture of tar and sand, has hardened around the rocks and is now very bumpy. The road is slated to be improved by the end of the year 2000 to match the quality of the road to Bahariya from Cairo.

In spite of its small size, this town is the site of two major archaeological digs. The first is at Ain el-Rees, which was and still is the largest spring of four in the area, around which were built a fortress, a church, a palace, a few cemeteries, and a wine factory (only recently discovered). The

second site is at Ain el-Ezza (*ain* means "spring"), where remains of a small village were found, along with tombs cut into nearby ridges and fragments of their mummies, which were robbed in ancient times. One can also see evidence of a system of aqueducts.

For years I have been especially interested in the site at Ain el-Rees, because I believe it was a Roman settlement, which means that it could serve as a window into every aspect of life during the transformation of Egyptian civilization at the end of antiquity. When I visited the site in 1993, the local Antiquities Inspectors and I worked an entire day just trying to distinguish the separate monuments at the site. The tops of the walls were slightly raised in certain areas, but for the most part they had disappeared beneath the sand. I collected pottery shards from the surface and examined the layout of the existing monuments.

The most prominent monument in El Haiz is the large fortress, two of whose walls still protrude from the top of a hill of sand overlooking the modern village. Dated to the Roman Period, the fortress was built mostly of mud bricks and apparently served as a garrison, the first line of defense against any attack from the desert. I believe that the Roman rulers and soldiers actually lived at the site.

On another knoll opposite the garrison, Fakhry found the remains of a large Coptic church. It originally consisted of two levels connected by staircases built of mud bricks, and its whitewashed walls were decorated with scenes, possibly, at the end of the fifth century, the early Coptic Period. Unfortunately, no paintings have survived at the site. In fact, gashes in the walls indicate

**The Roman fortress at El Haiz, the largest found in all the Egyptian oases**

*Opposite top:* **A fig tree on the outskirts of El Haiz, with the Roman fortress in the background. The settlement around the springs of Ain el-Rees would have been much larger during the Roman Period than it is now that the wells are gradually drying up.**

*Opposite bottom and page 148:* **The site of the Roman settlement at El Haiz at sunrise**

*Pages 146–47:* **Some of the subsidiary chapels surrounding the sanctuary, which were added to the Temple of Alexander the Great throughout the Roman Period.**

*Opposite and below:* The fortress, built on a mound of sandstone to protect the Oasis during the Roman Period, probably housed Roman soldiers who guarded this outpost of the Western Desert.

Interior of the Coptic church

*Right:* A stairway in the Coptic church leading from the narthex to the upper balcony overlooking the sanctuary, restored with mud brick similar to the ancient construction material

*Top:* One of the earliest Coptic churches built near the Roman monuments of El Haiz, now being conserved and restored by the Antiquities Department

The ancient well next to the Coptic church, probably used by some of the first Christian worshipers in the area

that some of the religious imagery—such as the crosses that probably hung there—was destroyed. The ancient church is currently being restored to its original beauty by local Moslems with the support of the Supreme Council of Antiquities, which seems fitting in light of the fact that a few of the famous mosques in Cairo had actually been built centuries ago by Coptic architects. The floor plan of the church is strikingly similar to modern cathedrals, which were clearly inspired by early models like this one. The main entrance is located on one side of the church and leads into a kind of foyer with alcoves carved into the walls, presumably for the placement of holy icons. The series of arches, reminiscent of Byzantine architecture, surround the once high-ceilinged central sanctuary. A staircase on each side of the narthex wound up to balconies that originally afforded a view of the sanctuary and the valley below. All of this was achieved with building materials much like those used locally today—mud bricks layered and then covered with a type of solidifying mud packed with dry straw. On the church grounds facing the town of El Haiz, a circle of stones still surrounds the original well, where residents come to fill their containers with fresh spring water today just as their predecessors did thousands of years ago.

Next to the church, Fakhry found the remains of a building that he believed was an even earlier place of Christian worship, used before Roman officials built the church. He described it as "decorated with primitive paintings of the faces of a bearded Christ and a large cross in the center of which is the head of Christ or a saint." He also found what he thought was an altar in the hallway, which may have been one of the original gathering places for local followers of Christ's teachings before the religion became institutionalized. Unfortunately, none of this remains.

The unexcavated Roman palace of El Haiz, situated next to the fortress

*Left:* An archaeological survey of the palace with its many hallways and colonnades shows it to be one of the largest of its kind in Egypt.

Our preliminary survey in 1993 of the area around the fortress revealed a maze of mud-brick walls covering four acres and the remains of a long wall surrounding the entire structure. From architectural features, I concluded that this was a very large Roman palace, the likes of which we have not yet seen in Egypt. Although we cannot fully understand the structure until the excavation is complete, we can see that the walls were covered inside and out with plaster and painted with hunting scenes and green, yellow, and red plants. The remains of a long row of columns also reveal painted scenes. The fortress itself would have served as a garrison for soldiers who were present to defend against revolution or attack and also to protect the region's ruler, who would have lived in the palace. Once the rooms are fully excavated, the architecture and frescoes will greatly enrich our knowledge of this Roman settlement.

The residence of the Egyptian king, or royal palace, was known as the *per-aa*, which means "Great House" and is the origin of the word "pharaoh." The structure and use of palaces varied through the centuries, and they have not been particularly well preserved. However, the most impressive examples are the palace of Akhenaten at El Amarna, the palace of Ramses II within the Ramesseum at Western Thebes, and the palace of Merenptah at Memphis. The tombs of pharaohs were considered symbolic palaces and were decorated with painted images of palace life, including intimate family scenes, the king's activities both in and outside of Egypt, hunting and battle scenes, water gardens, and wildlife.

Down the hill from the palace at El Haiz is a large Roman cemetery whose tombs are cut into the sandstone. (Cemeteries were always located south of dwellings because the winds generally blow

**The changing of the guards at El Haiz at sunset**

from the north, carrying sand with them.) Part of the cemetery was excavated in 1900 by Georg Steindorff. During our initial survey and excavation at this site, Inspector Mohammed Aiady discovered three tiny gold amulets. Another large Roman cemetery with sandstone tombs is located only about three miles south of Ain el-Rees in the town of El Khabra. We can be sure that the tombs there hold many more artifacts, but in the meantime we can conclude that the soldiers who lived in the fortress were buried in the cemeteries near the palace, while the Valley of the Golden Mummies would have been used by civilians living in Bahariya. Perhaps the most interesting find at El Haiz was a structure that I believe was once a wine factory; this will be discussed in detail in chapter 11.

In the future, we plan to excavate the palace and the surrounding cemetery at El Haiz, an area that we believe was inhabited by Romans, Egyptians, and Egyptian Christians. By excavating the palace and cemetery, we hope to obtain information regarding the transition to Christianity and to explore the paleopathology of the people who lived during that time. It is possible that we may find evidence of diseases, such as leprosy, which have been alluded to in surviving Christian documents.

# THE WINE FACTORY

OST PEOPLE ASSOCIATE ANCIENT EGYPTIANS WITH TOMBS, TEMPLES, and pyramids and thus imagine that they were very serious people who were obsessed with death. We do not usually think of them as wine and beer drinkers celebrating and feasting, as we picture the ancient Greeks or Romans doing. It may be surprising, therefore, to learn that the grapevine was the most important cultivated plant in ancient Egypt and that wine was at one time its most popular export.

ANCIENT WINE PRODUCTION  Wine consumption and trade from one region to another were so widespread that wine is mentioned in *The Pyramid Texts* and depicted in many temple scenes. Sealed wine vessels still containing wine have been found dating as far back as the First Dynasty (3100–2890 B.C.), and pottery shards with wine residue date to the Predynastic Period. So we know the Egyptians have been producing and enjoying wine for at least five thousand years. Wine and its effects even played a significant role in their religious belief system.

The ancients believed that wine was imbued with its own sacred power, so they offered it to the deceased in order that he might be empowered and appear righteous before the gods in the Hall of Judgment. Wine also served as a symbol of eternity, probably because of the way grapes grew so abundantly in certain areas and gave new life to those who drank of their juice. Large jars of wine were also prepared as offerings to gods, another reason why we often find so many full wine jugs in tombs.

According to legend, the first Egyptian to discover the grapevine and make wine from it was the god Osiris, who became known in some areas as the Lord of Wine, among many other titles. A lesser-known god named Ssmw specifically ruled over wine, oil, and wineries, and the drinking of wine was connected with other gods, including Bes, the god of pleasure, who is sometimes shown drinking from large wine vessels. Worshipers are said to have drunk wine in the temples of Hathor during rituals because wine was believed to relax this important cowgoddess. Wine may also have been used ritualistically at the Festival of Bastet where, Herodotus noted, the cat-goddess was regularly intoxicated. Wine served an important function in efforts to transform Sekhmet, the destructive lioness-goddess, into a peaceful and more benevolent deity. The Greeks, of course, connected wine consumption and states of ecstasy with their god Dionysos, the Romans with Bacchus.

Wine was offered daily to the ancient gods as part of temple rituals. Pharaohs from the Sixth Dynasty through the end of the Greco-Roman Period are depicted in statues and temple wall paintings with large wine vessels in each hand, offering them to the gods. From religious songs in Ptolemaic temple paintings we know that wine was thought to give life to the *ka* and could thus

*Right and opposite:* The New Kingdom tomb of Sennefer in Luxor is called the "Tomb of the Grapes" for its depictions of various types of grapes.

*Opposite bottom:* An intact wine jar inscribed with the face of Bes, the Egyptian god of pleasure, found among many pottery shards in one of the tombs in the Valley of the Golden Mummies, where wine vessels were often left as offerings to the gods and also for the deceased's use in the afterlife

*Page 158:* The ceiling of the tomb of Sennefer was left roughly cut, so that the paintings of grapevines hung down to give it the effect of a real vineyard.

be used to attain immortality. Tombs were often decorated with scenes of activities considered dearest to the heart of the deceased; the Theban tomb of Djeserkaraseneb, for example, contains an elegant painting of guests at a banquet drinking so much that they show signs of sickness. On a wall of the tomb of Paheri in the wine region of El Kab, a woman at a feast says, "Give me eighteen cups of wine, for I wish to drink until drunkenness; my inside is like straw." Djeserkaraseneb and Paheri must have loved to give parties and considered it a great sign of abundance and joy when their guests drank to excess of their wine supply.

The ancients harvested at least three different types of grapes—red, white, and black (or very dark red)—all of which they ate as fresh fruit, dried to make raisins, and processed to make wine. They used the grape leaves in preparing food and also as lids to seal wine vessels. Grapes,

in both their natural and fermented states, were employed for curative purposes and were often a basic ingredient in medications. Grape leaves found inside a mummy in Hawara dating to Greco-Roman times are now in the Agricultural Museum in Cairo.

The Egyptian word for grape wine, *Irp*, refers to the fermentation process. Wine was so central to Egyptian life that each region was known for its particular type. Five kinds, each representing a different area, are noted as superior in *The Pyramid Texts*. Lower Egypt was said to have produced the best-quality wine, referred to as *imat*, possibly from the town of Buto, and *snw*, the wine of Tell el-Farma, was also renowned. Other popular wines included *prhbyt*, from Bahbeit, El Hagara in Lower Egypt, Tell-Defna, Abusir, and Mariut, whose wine was dedicated to the god Osiris. The famous Old Kingdom capital city of Memphis was also known for its grape wine.

The Harris Papyrus tells us that farmers in the areas around the western oases took good care of their grapevines and that the regions of Quft, El Kab, Elephantine, and Nubia also produced wines. By the Sixth Dynasty and the First Intermediate Period (c. 2345–2055 B.C.), texts began to include references to *prpsnc*, a wine from the south, and during the New Kingdom, the wines of Upper Egypt and Nubia gained some notoriety. In a papyrus of the third century A.D., Pliny, the Roman historian, suggests that pomegranate was included in the liquid mixture. He

also corroborates the use of three special wines that appear in ancient funerary and offering texts.

The stages of wine production itself can be understood not only from temple walls but also from actual wineries discovered primarily in Lower Egypt. A progression of early painted wall scenes depict a simple process: first, the grapes were picked from vines and transported in baskets to a place where they were sorted and washed. Wine makers would stamp the grapes with their feet, and the resulting juice was then poured into vessels and left to ferment. Scenes from New Kingdom temples indicate that the process had become more sophisticated. Instead of baskets, grapes were collected in basins with spouts. The pressing of grapes with the feet began to disappear, and the operation was conducted after sunset so that the sun's rays would not evaporate the liquid.

Archaeologists have found many ancient wine factories near the city of Alexandria, the region best known for its wine exports. Examples excavated at Abu-Mina, Kom Trouga, and the city of Marina all date to the late Roman and early Byzantine Periods, and from these sites archaeologists have been able to distinguish between two basic types of presses. One is a small, portable basin, like a tub, in which grapes were crushed, with a spout on the side of the basin through which the juice could be poured into smaller vessels. The other press is more like a vat with plaster-covered walls, so that the grape juice could remain fermenting in the basin for as long as desired without seeping through the walls. The Abu-Mina factory has a good example of the latter type of basin, which had a fitted wooden cover and where the fermenting wine could remain on site rather than being transported elsewhere for the fermentation process. In wineries found at Kom Trouga, the rooms used for pressing the grapes have a completely sealed, vaulted ceiling to prevent contamination from dust and to keep other ingredients from affecting the pure juice. The ceiling also served to regulate the temperature so that juice would ferment more rapidly in warm weather.

Two wineries were found in Marina, one of them with a third type of press for squeezing the grapes, which involved the use of two basins with spouts that led into a third basin, where two types of juice could be combined, perhaps to create a new kind of wine. The second wine factory excavated in Marina was even more sophisticated. A mastaba, or bench, built in the form of a quarter circle, was fitted into each corner of the basin to store the wine vessels after filling. Small holes in the floors were designed to collect the leftover seeds and skins.

The Greeks and Romans in Egypt experimented with ingredients to enhance and vary the taste and types of wine produced. Egg whites were used to make a very pure white wine; the use of heat during fermentation also helped to purify the juice and kept it fresh for much longer. The addition of yeast seemed to make the end result clearer and brighter. Seawater, flowers, and natural herbs indigenous to Egypt must have also lent a unique taste and smell to these wines. The Greek wines were relatively sweet; resin, used to seal the amphoras, gave the wine a distinctive taste.

During the Roman Period, the wines most highly favored by Egyptians came from the Kharga and Dakhla Oases, but wine making was an important part of daily life in all the oases. Bahariya was well known from ancient times for its range of wines made from two types of grapes, which still grow in the Oasis—white and red varietals, each with large seeds—and for its sweet date wine. Seals from wine jugs inscribed with the mark of Bahariya have been found as far away as El Amarna, the capital of Egypt during the reign of Akhenaten (1352–1336 B.C.), and wall

carvings in various parts of Egypt refer to wine from Bahariya. The residents enjoyed making wine and drinking it in abundance, and of course they prospered from the riches that came from its trade and export. Wine was the principal export of Bahariya Oasis at this time and part of the reason its inhabitants accrued enough wealth to be gilded at their burial. Bahariya's wines caused it to become an important commercial center, which no doubt made it an appealing place for foreigners to settle.

The Roman residents were so particular about their wine that they made a distinction between the products made from the first or second picking within a season. Some preferred the ripest grapes taken off the vine first, which produced a wine that was bottled and labeled differently from wines made from the second and third harvests. The highest-quality wine seems to have been made with juice compressed from grapes and left to ferment in a storage vessel. Water was added to grapes of the second harvest as they were squeezed through a press with a wooden lid. The third class of wine, considered the drink of the poor, was a mixture of water and juice squeezed from the skin and seeds left at the bottom of the compressor. The wine makers of Bahariya left their wine in jars sealed with wax lids for at least six months to complete fermentation; sometimes the jars were stored for as long as three to four years, though if wine were kept any longer than this, it turned into vinegar. New wines were opened during the Festival of the Opening of the Vessels each spring and were usually filtered through a cloth as they were poured out.

Because of its high quality, Bahariya wine was considered an excellent gift during the New Kingdom and became one of the favorite Egyptian wines during the Greco-Roman Period. Seals or stamps inscribed with the name *irp n wḥ³t* (meaning "wine from the oasis") and pressed into wine vessels have been found even at Tell el-Amarna. As we have seen, the word for Bahariya wine, *DjesDjes*, eventually became synonymous with the region itself.

## THE WINE FACTORY AT EL HAIZ

This rich history of wine production and trade explains why one of the most exciting results of our recent survey of El Haiz was the unexpected discovery about 1988, by the Antiquities Inspectors in Bahariya, of an ancient wine factory just west of the Roman fortress, near the boundaries of the palace. The factory can be dated

to the Roman Period and would have served the palace and fortress, providing the soldiers with an ample supply of wine. I consider this discovery one of the most important in Bahariya, because this is the first wine factory ever found here, and it enables us to confirm the widespread fame that the Oasis claimed for its wine from pharaonic through Roman times.

The layout of this unique structure is similar to that of ancient Roman baths, as well as Islamic baths still in use in Cairo. The existence of hot springs directly underneath the area once occupied by the building suggests the possibility that it could have been a bathhouse, whose basins were once filled with water of different temperatures. However, the presence of many broken wine vessels and countless grape seeds within the borders of the structure confirms for me that it was indeed used for making wine. We have uncovered here nearly all of the factory's architectural components except for the west side, which was partially lost during the excavation because of the inexperience of some of the workers and the lack of supervision. To insure a more scientific excavation, I sent Mansour Boriak to oversee the workers, while I continued to work in the Valley of the Golden Mummies.

The building was constructed of mud-brick walls on a foundation cut into the sandstone. The walls were encased in a very thick layer of plaster, remnants of which still cover several sections; the plaster would have kept the grape juice and wine from being absorbed into the walls during fermentation. The largest room, which is located in the northwest corner of the building and was found without a ceiling, is probably where the grapes were collected and cleaned with water. After selecting the good-quality grapes, sorting them by type, and discarding the rest, the ancient wine makers would have carried the usable crop to separate processing rooms according to their type.

The first processing room that we found appears to be about twelve feet square with a depth of about ten feet and walls about two feet thick. The room contains a hollow area in the center, in which the grapes would have been pressed, and the floor appears to slope to allow the juice to flow out. On the wall opposite the collecting room is a hole that was probably a spout that

*Opposite top:* The author documenting the partially excavated wine factory on the site at El Haiz. The room in the foreground was used in Greco-Roman times to collect the grape juice after compressing and before fermentation.

*Opposite bottom:* Ancient grape seeds and pottery shards found in the rooms at the wine factory of El Haiz. The substance on the bottom of the wine vessel and around its mouth is either residue from the ancient wine or resin applied to the inside of the vessels as a sealant.

*Below:* The author stands with his Antiquities Inspectors at the outer edge of the wine factory, whose walls were all covered with plaster to keep the juice from soaking through the mud brick.

The largest room in the wine factory was used to collect and wash the two types of grapes, which would then be sorted and moved to another room for pressing.

carried the wine from the compressor through a narrow channel into a collector basin. A semi-circular mastaba in the corner of the room may have been used to hold containers of grapes or juice. Preliminary evidence suggests that the juice was transported to three different basins through a series of spouts and channels, and that the resulting mixtures were then processed to make different types of wine. Although unexcavated, a second collector basin seems to lie directly west of the first and has a lip that could have been used to hold a wooden cover to protect the wine. This basin also has a bench like that in the first basin. A third basin, which is located next to the others, is the same in every respect except that it contained the ashes of burned plants, indicating that this type of wine must have been fermented by heating.

The excavation of each section of this vast settlement of El Haiz will, as always, require patience, persistence, and much funding (which itself requires patience and persistence to obtain!), but it is a project that I anticipate happily. I expect that the results of our team's excavations in El Haiz will answer a range of questions that have intrigued Egyptian, Greek, and Roman scholars for many years.

DATE WINE   Another product for which Bahariya became famous was its uniquely sweet wine made from a special type of date that grows in the region and could be fermented. The freshly picked dates would be soaked in water with yeast, pressed, and then left to ferment in sealed jars. Date trees conveyed status on those who grew them in private gardens, and they can still be found in the yards of many villagers in El Bawiti. Not only do they lend dignity to the house, but the type of date indigenous to Bahariya is also said to contain a desirable substance that fosters relaxation.

Several sources have recorded the various ways in which date trees were integral to daily life in the western oases. Traces of date trees have been found in Kharga Oasis, indicating their presence

On a wall of the New Kingdom tomb of Ba-Shedu at Deir el-Medinah, the deceased is seen worshiping a sacred palm tree heavy with ripe dates, a tree associated with the goddesses Isis and Hathor.

*Below left:* Ripe dates are ready for picking on a farm in El Bawiti.

*Below right:* A boy rides his donkey through a grove of date palms. Dates are still the main agricultural product of Bahariya Oasis.

as far back as the Stone Age, and mummies interred there were covered with mats made from date-palm fronds. The tying of long palm leaves into a circle was a powerful symbol of union for ancient Egyptians, and we can tell from the scenes on tomb walls that mourners of the dead carried palm fronds in funeral processions and threw them down on the road before the deceased on the way to be buried. Today, Egyptians still plant palm leaves on graves as an offering to the deceased. There were several types of edible dates, of which only a few were fermented into the famous sweet wine that Bahariya Oasis exported to the Nile Valley in great quantities.

# THE TEMPLE OF BES

IN JULY 1988 A RESIDENT OF EL BAWITI CAME TO THE ANTIQUITIES INSPECTORATE at Bahariya and handed over a piece of basalt carved with the cartouche of Akhenaten. This is the only artifact found at Bahariya that refers to this pharaoh, who was commonly known as the "heretic king" because he rejected polytheism for the worship of the single god Aten. Egyptian law requires that ancient artifacts be preserved, not sold, and anyone who can guide us to antiquities is rewarded. The man who found the stone eagerly led us to a small tell, or mound of ruins, among the houses of El Bawiti, where he said the inscribed stone had just been lying in the dust. The following month, Ashry Shaker began a systematic excavation of this site and uncovered a unique ancient temple, the only one known to be dedicated to Bes, the god of pleasure, sexuality, dancing, wine, and music, as well as and the protector of mothers and children.

During the excavation, it became clear that the temple had been partially destroyed in the early Christian period. The area was reduced to a mound of rubble and was quarried by local builders for *tafla*, the desert clay used to make mud bricks for houses. The temple's construction dates to the Ptolemaic Period, but we know from artifacts found inside that it was in use until the fourth century A.D. The temple served Bes in his aspect as the god of grape and date wines, which were the most important products of Bahariya Oasis at that time.

This particular god provides a good example of how religious iconography was gradually transformed from one dynasty to the next. The cult of Bes became popular in the New Kingdom, but his origins can be traced back to the Old Kingdom, when he was depicted in association with fertility, circumcision, and harvest rituals. At that time he was represented in a somewhat simplistic style with slender, flexed legs and holding serpents over his head. His role developed in the Middle Kingdom into that of guardian of the home, infants, and new mothers, and in this manifestation he often assisted Taweret, the hippopotamus-goddess of pregnancy, in protecting women during childbirth. His designation expanded to include joy, sexuality, and pleasurable pursuits, and he was often pictured as a dwarf, holding drums or tambourines, playing the flute, and dancing. By the Late and Greco-Roman Periods, Bes was shown with a menacing countenance, brandishing knives and swords, an indication that his role as protector now extended to warfare against evil forces. In earlier times Bes's physical features were used to denote at least ten different gods, including Aha, Amam, Hayet, Ihty, Mefdjet, Menew, Segen, Soped, and Tetetenu, but over the centuries the identity and images of all these deities were incorporated into the composite god Bes.

The appearance of Bes's fearsome image on amulets and magic knives (symbolic weapons inscribed with figures of deities and mythical animals) in the New Kingdom indicates his popularity at that time, particularly during the Eighteenth Dynasty. Bes also appears on a frieze in the

A narrow alley between the houses of El Bawiti, similar to the one where the inscribed basalt fragment found by a local villager led archaeologists to the Temple of Bes

*Below:* Plan of the Temple of Bes

*Page 168:* The largest statue of Bes ever found in Egypt, this figure is four feet high.

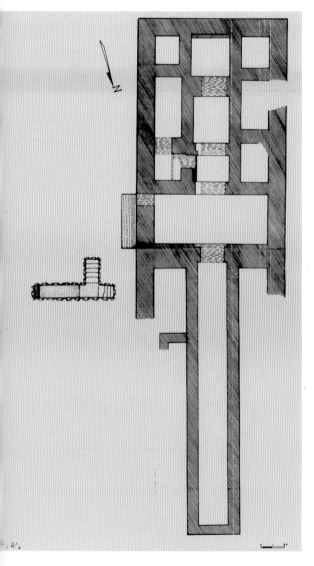

palace of the Eighteenth Dynasty king Amenhotep III at Malkata, on the walls of some houses in the workmen's villages at El Amarna in Middle Egypt, and at Deir el-Medina on the west bank of Luxor. In the Greco-Roman Period, Bes was featured in the *mammisi,* or birth houses, which were always located next to major temples, such as the Ptolemaic temple at El Amarna and the Roman-built Temple of Hathor at Dendara.

It has long been debated whether Bes was a native creation of the Egyptian imagination or imported from another culture. A few distinguishing features have brought his indigenous origin into question. First, the impassive profiles and idealized features of all other Egyptian deities were not used for Bes, who was depicted head-on with exaggerated facial features. Unlike the other, slender gods, Bes was represented as an undignified, squat figure with bandy legs and the ears and mane of a lion; he was usually shown naked except for a headdress of tall plumes. In several inscriptions he is referred to as the Lord of Punt, a territory far south of Egypt on the African coast. Some archaeologists believe this association may be explained by an expedition to Punt made by Harkhouf, a governor of Aswan. An inscription carved on the walls of Harkhouf's tomb indicates that he returned from Punt and the lands to the south with a pygmy for Pepy II, a Sixth Dynasty ruler. Egyptians were thus familiar from about 2200 B.C. with the pygmies of Central Africa, and some scholars suggest that this awareness may account for Bes's short, stocky build.

Some Egyptologists concluded that Bes's feathered headdress, full lips, and broad, flat nose are similar to traits found in Nubia, indicating that his image was derived from this region south of Egypt, but these claims have been discredited, because other deities, such as Hathor, whose native origins have never been in dispute, have also been depicted head-on and referred to as the "Lord of Punt." And early versions of the lion-man image have been found in Old Kingdom

The remains of the Temple of Bes, god of pleasure, wine, fertility, and childbirth, who was especially revered during the Greco-Roman Period and was a favored deity in Bahariya

*Below:* The main interior hallway leading to the sanctuary and chapels in the Temple of Bes, the only temple dedicated to this god in all of Egypt

examples long before the influence of foreign cultures. The Bes image is therefore now considered purely Egyptian.

During the Greco-Roman Period, as we have seen, Bahariya Oasis prospered as a military outpost and an important center of wine production, an activity with which Bes was often associated. The fact that wine making and wine consumption were so central to life in the Oasis at that time accounts for its being the site of the only existing temple of Bes. There is evidence that he was worshiped in several locations in Bahariya in addition to El Bawiti. During the excavations at Ain el-Muftella near El Qasr in 1939, for example, Ahmed Fakhry uncovered four ruined chapels; in the third chapel oversized figures of Bes were carved into each wall (see chapter 14). Our recent

One of the rooms in the sanctuary area where archaeologists uncovered the statue of Bes

*Below:* The figure of Bes, carved in sandstone and painted, is depicted as a naked dwarf with a lion's head and a feathered crown.

excavations at the newly discovered temple site have uncovered the largest known statue of Bes and a number of wall paintings.

The original architecture and plan of the temple of Bes are similar to those of other Greco-Roman temples in Egypt, which employed the Egyptian rather than Roman style. The entire structure, which is made of mud bricks on a foundation of limestone blocks, measures nearly sixty by forty feet. It lies on a north-south axis with a causeway or ramp, which was most likely lined with sphinxes, leading to its north entrance. In a long, horizontal hall with a stucco floor, the entrance for worshipers, a statue of Bes was found in three pieces lying in front of its base. The copper vessels strewn around the statue may have been used to present incense and offerings to the god. A small door off the main hallway led down a short ramp to a rock-cut water shaft, where the ancients apparently used the water to cure illnesses.

The statue of Bes is also one of the best preserved ever found. It is about four feet high, carved with well-defined features that still bear traces of its original colors. His image from the front is typical of the Ptolemaic Period. More dwarflike than leonine, Bes is shown with short, squat legs, hunched shoulders, and a rounded stomach; he is naked except for a belt that curves below his belly and what appears to be a monkey skin over his back. Bes's leonine qualities are still evident, in the facial features, ears, and mane, but the paws on his shoulders and thighs and the tail that hangs down to the floor in back are clearly those of a monkey skin draped over his back, not that of a lion. On Bes's head is a tall headdress of plumes bound with a horizontal band. The god's face is clearly defined by large eyes, a flat nose, and a wide-open mouth with twelve teeth and a protruding tongue. His curling beard resembles the mane of a lion, and on his chest he wears an amulet of the bull Serapis. The hair on the back of his head resembles a handkerchief that ends in a knot falling down over the statue's back. His hands rest on his thighs, which are open to reveal his penis.

Behind the public hall of worship were private rooms reserved for temple personnel or priests and a large sanctuary. Evidence shows, however, that these were additions and modifications made at the end of the Roman Period, when the two main halls located behind the public hall were converted into nine smaller rooms in three rows of three. Remains of the sphinx statues along the causeway, a typical feature in temples of the New Kingdom and later, appear to have been intentionally destroyed, probably to encourage worshipers of Bes to convert to Christianity.

Several artifacts were discovered in these temple rooms. They include one faience *shabti* made in the form of a person wearing a tight dress and a royal false beard. The hands cross over the chest and a tightened fist holds a tool in the shape of the hieroglyphic sign meaning "pyramid," the style of which is typical of the Greco-Roman Period. Another amulet of red copper depicts a seated cat, and a miniature statuette of Horus is evidence of the detailed workmanship and dedication still shown this important god during the Greek and Roman occupation. A circular game board of sandstone is carved with two concentric circles, each with several depressions into which gaming pieces could be placed and moved; a die with the numbers one through six on its six faces was also uncovered. Two copper bowls, one decorated with plants, were probably used for wine or oil, and another copper dish standing on three cowlike legs may have served as an incense burner. A pottery bowl made of red Nile clay dates to the third or fourth century A.D.

Because Bes is often associated with wine and the Oasis was a major wine producer and exporter, it is clear that he was important enough to the people of Bahariya to have a temple dedicated to him. When they came during the Feast of Bes to leave offerings in front of his temple, they most likely shared with him an ample supply of their best local wines.

**Detail showing the unusual back side of the god, with the skin of a monkey**

*Below:* **Detail of the head of Bes**

# THE TEMPLE
# OF HERCULES

O NE DAY IN OCTOBER 1996, WHEN FARAG ALLAH ABDEEN, AN ANTIQUITIES
Inspector at Bahariya, was walking in a desert area south of the town of El Bawiti, he found on
the surface of the sand a few pottery shards and broken stones. He submitted a report of his findings to Ashry Shaker, who informed me. Shortly afterward, the Bahariya office received enough
funding for a preliminary survey of the site and one season of excavation. A small team worked
from the beginning of January through the end of June 1997 and was able to uncover the shat-
tered remains of what was indisputably a Roman temple, although the workers could not determine to whom it had been dedicated. The most important aspect of the discovery were the
twenty-seven stelae (inscribed stone slabs) they found strewn around the temple floors, each
inscribed in the hieratic and demotic Egyptian scripts, as well as in Greek. This is the first time
such a large number of stelae from this period inscribed in this fashion have been recovered from
an Egyptian oasis. A clearer understanding of the temple's significance, I soon realized, would
require the corroboration of a specialist in the ancient Greek language, so I asked Dr. Frederic
Colin of the French Archaeological Institute to help translate the inscriptions, and then I went with
my own team to excavate the area further during the winter digging season of 1999.

There are still signs of a road that once led from the south to the temple entrance. We cannot be sure what form the temple gate took, although we can tell that it must have been very large,
because two thick walls of mud brick on a foundation of sandstone blocks on each side of the
entry corridor span a gap of nearly ten feet. The temple itself is almost completely destroyed, but
from its surviving ruins we can still get a detailed idea of what it looked like almost two thousand years ago. Worshipers would have walked up a short set of steps from the road to enter a
long, rectangular hall from the south in front of the sanctuary. Priests would have been the only
ones permitted to enter the sanctuary, which they did by a series of steps on the northwest side.
A wall surrounding the entire temple, with bases that probably held a series of sphinxes, was built
during the Roman Period from mud bricks and blocks cut from local sandstone. This exterior
wall would have been covered with a thick layer of white plaster, some of which can still be seen
on the sanctuary walls. Additions to the original structure built later in the Roman Period included
more chapels off to each side of the sanctuary.

What remains of the slightly curved western wall around the temple is connected to the
outside steps; three lower walls that branch off to the west could have served as bases for statues
of goddesses decorating the road that led to the temple. The sanctuary is divided into three chapels
which we designated Chapels A, B, and C. The largest chapel, in the middle, Chapel B, contained
all the clues that led us to believe this temple was dedicated to the worship of Hercules. Like

**Plan of the Temple of Hercules**

*Below:* The mud-brick walls of the inner sanctuary are still partially covered with plaster.

*Page 174:* The remains of the Temple of Hercules built of mud brick on a sandstone foundation over 2,000 years ago while the Greeks ruled Egypt

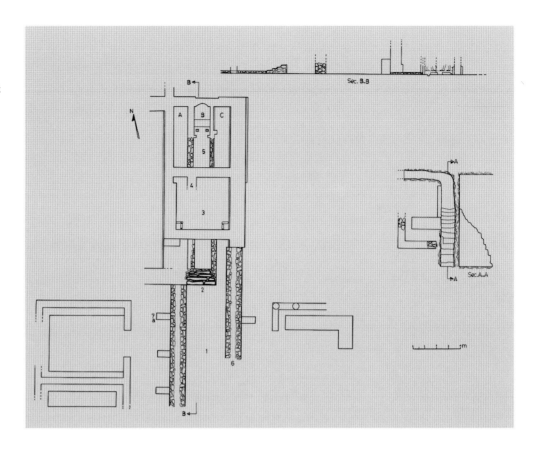

Achilles and other Greek heroes, Herakles (called Hercules by the Romans) was worshiped as a godlike figure; the cult of Hercules was especially popular in Egypt, where he was a symbol of power and a defender in wartime.

Square sockets carved into the rock floor of Chapel B allowed us to imagine that a wooden door, hinged to the floor, served as its formal entrance. The white plaster encasing the entrance is much thicker here than in the other chapels, indicating the special importance given to the deity worshiped in the main chapel. Other unique features of the structure, which demonstrate that particular care was taken in its construction, are the two tall blocks that form the frame of the entrance to the sanctuary and the Greek inscriptions found below them on sandstone stelae. One can still see on the main chapel's interior walls the carved bas-relief legs and feet of an emperor, probably Octavian Augustus, who ordered the construction of the temple. In front of the figure, facing the ruler, are two sets of carved male legs painted dark red. One of the men must have been Hercules, to whom the king was making offerings; the other was most likely an Egyptian deity. Chapel B shows evidence of having had a vaulted ceiling, while the other two chapels had standard flat ceilings. Chapel C, to the east, is slightly smaller than the others. In Chapel A, there are vestiges of an oven that still contains ashes and may have been used to prepare fresh offerings. Next to the oven a pile of dried date pits could be the leftovers of numerous offerings made to Hercules in an effort to perpetuate the abundance of the Oasis's produce.

A few rooms were added to the temple at a later date to serve practical purposes. A rectangular room next to the west wall is mostly lost now, but in its center is a smaller room that may have been used to provide the temple with water. To the east, a separate building, fronted by two mud-brick columns encased in plaster, would have been a suitable residence for the presiding high priest. About a mile to the southwest is a large rock-cut tomb with Greek inscriptions, possibly a sacred burial site used during later Roman times.

An archaeologist from the excavation team, Aiman Wahby, points out the sockets in the floor of the Temple of Hercules where a door once served as the formal entrance to Chapel B, which contains relief carvings of Hercules, the hero revered in Egypt during the Greco-Roman Period.

*Below:* Epigrapher Noha Abdul Hafiz works inside the main sanctuary of the Temple of Hercules. Stelae with Greek inscriptions were discovered in the surrounding area, which will be excavated in the future.

**One of the sandstone stelae inscribed with Greek writing found within the Temple of Hercules**

The twenty-seven sandstone stelae were found dispersed throughout the main sanctuary and inside a hole fronting the sanctuary, most likely the result of Christian sabotage. But at one time these stelae must have been hung on the interior walls, similar to those found by the French archaeologist Auguste Mariette inside the Serapeum at Saqqara in 1851. The stelae at El Haiz represent offerings of prayers made to an array of Greek and Egyptian gods, including Amun, who was for the Greeks the Egyptian equivalent of Hercules. Deities other than Hercules mentioned in the stelae, and therefore worshiped in this temple, include Pantheos, Ra, Horus, Khonsu, Apollo, and Hermes. It is possible that still more gods were favored recipients of the locals' entreaties, but some of the inscriptions are so damaged that they cannot be fully deciphered.

The inscriptions on the stelae, as translated in their entirety from the Greek by Dr. Colin, read as follows:

I, Gorgias, son of Dionysos, came to the helpful Herakles, after having made a wish.

I . . . son of Demetrios, scribe, came to all the gods and to Herakles. Also made in the name of Ptolemas and Tiphon.

Good luck. On the year 18th, on the 17th of Tybi, I, Didymos, son of Herakleites, grandson of Kephalas, came to Herakles and to all the gods, after having made a wish. On the year 19th, on the 2nd of Tybi, I, Thessalos, son of Herakleites, came to the Pantheos, after having made a wish.

To Amun and to Herakles, god who listen the prayer, Petechon, son of Hippalos, the Libyan, made this inscription for Agathokles and for his mother, Eutychia.

Petechonsis, son of Petobastis . . . Chonsis, the greatest god, after having made a wish.

On the year . . . on the 17 of Tybi, Apollonios, son of Artemidoros, came to the Pantheos.

. . . on the year . . . on the 6th of Tybi, I, Artemidoros, son of Apollonios, came to . . .

I . . . son of Didymos, came to the gods who are living here, after having made a wish.

On the 22th, on the 10th of Phaophi, Chonsis made his inscription for the greatest gods.

I, Pachos, son of Pachos, came to the helpful Amun and . . .

On the year 21th, on the 20th of Tybi, I Petechon, son of Hippalos, made this inscription for myself, and for my father, and for my mother.

Rachte, Thailloi

I, Didymos, son of Hermokles.

The name of NN is written here in front of . . . and of Amun, and of the gods who are living here all together.

Amun-Ra'Hor and Khonsu, the great god, lord of Djesdjes, might they give life to the prophet . . . son of the prophet Anch-hor and of . . .

Ptollis, son of Ammonios, made up this inscription.

To Apollon, Herm . . .

. . . I came to all the gods. Ptolemaios.

The 9th day of Pachon, I, Ptollis, son of Aristodelos, came to the gods who are living here after having made a wish. Petobastis, son of Heribastet and of Tati, has written.

. . . on the year 10th, the 20th of Kaisereion.

Words said by Khonsu.

. . . I came to the gods who are living here after having made a wish.

One inscription is illegible, and the demotic inscriptions have not yet been translated, but we believe they will be the same as the Greek text.

When the Greeks settled in Egypt during the Twenty-sixth Dynasty, they built temples dedicated to specific gods or goddesses associated with the areas in which the temples were located. Onto the prevailing local Egyptian deities they overlaid corresponding Greek gods and goddesses who had the same function. For example, they worshiped the image of Amun but in their minds he was Zeus, so they came to know him as Amun-Zeus. Similarly, Demeter was worshiped as Isis and Hathor. In addition to giving Egyptian gods Greek names, they also gave Greek gods Egyptian names. Hercules was often worshiped by his Egyptian name, Hry shef, meaning Lord of the Desert, protector of the borders. Hry shef is depicted as a ram-headed figure in the necropolis at Ihnasya el-Medinah in Fayum, where residents renamed their city Herakleopolis Magna, meaning "great city of Hercules" after he became their primary sacred hero. The cult of Hercules was important in the oases. In Siwa Oasis he was worshiped as Hry shef, but in Bahariya Oasis, he was worshiped by his Greek name. Herodotus wrote that the moon-god Khonsu, son of Amun, was also known as Herakles in Egypt and referred to him as "Herakles-Khonsu." One day, the god Amun appeared to Herodotus in a dream with the head of a ram, which meant that Amun too was associated with Herakles. These are just a few of the myriad examples in which Greek and Egyptian gods had merged.

The artifacts found inside the Temple of Hercules represent a diverse array of gods. A statue of Thoth as a baboon was found in two parts and has now been restored. He sits on a chair without pillars, his hands on his legs; black paint remains on his eyes and mouth, and nearly half of the tail is still attached. The artist took care to add details to the legs and even separated some of the fingers. Also found in the temple were a small statuette of a cow-headed Hathor and a stone carving of Horus.

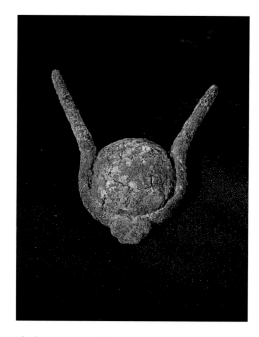

The bronze crown of Hathor, goddess of love and beauty, is often depicted with cow horns holding a sun disk. This is a fragment of a votive statue found in the Temple of Hercules.

*Below:* This sandstone statue of a lion found inside the temple resembles the sphinxes of ancient Egypt.

A unique twelve-inch statue of Hercules is a clear example of the major stylistic differences between depictions of Greek and Egyptian deities. Detailed facial features reveal a strong jaw and thick hair, similar to the Hellenistic style in which Alexander the Great was often rendered. The left ear was carved outside the bushy mane, while the right ear is hidden. No longer were Greek sculptors concerned with the aesthetics of symmetry, nor did they show the care that the Egyptian artisans did in achieving balance in all things. The Greeks instead had an eye for detail and personal expressiveness, which can be seen in the small smile, eyes, and nose of Hercules, modeled in a very different style from the staring Egyptian Thoth.

The terra-cotta head of a bull found on the site is probably a depiction of Serapis, an Egyptian deity widely praised by the Greeks and Romans. Also found were a pottery lamp with no inscriptions, a horse's head made of terra cotta, and a strangely shaped and decorated pottery vessel. We believe that this must be an ancient wine vessel, although the style is unlike anything I have ever seen. It consists of a hollow pipe connected at both ends to form a circle with four holes on top, through which wine was poured and possibly mixed. The vessel is decorated with dots, which may represent grape seeds, and a nude Greek god drawn to look like Dionysos.

From our study of the inscriptions found inside the sanctuary, I believe that this temple may date from 21 B.C., during the reign of Octavian Augustus (30 B.C.–A.D. 14), first of the Roman rulers, and was used until the second century A.D. It appears to have been deliberately damaged during the Christian era. The architecture and the stelae make this a unique temple in Egypt and one of exceptional importance in providing us with further clues about the interaction between Egyptian, Greek, and Roman religions and rulership during this time period.

The fact that a site of this importance can be discovered simply by accident, not on the basis of prior research, proves that Bahariya is practically a virgin archaeological site. I fully expect that a more thorough excavation and study of the Temple of Hercules and its immediate surroundings when we return next season will reveal much more about the worship of this Greek deity alongside his Egyptian counterparts.

Epigrapher Noha Abdul Hafiz, traces the few remaining inscriptions left behind on the walls of the Temple of Hercules.

*Opposite:* Two bronze statuettes found in the Temple of Hercules—one of the god Osiris as a mummy with crossed arms; the other of the Greek goddess Aphrodite wearing the crown of Hathor—offer a good example of how images of Greek and Egyptian deities sometimes merged.

# OTHER BAHARIYA
# TEMPLES AND TOMBS

BAHARIYA OASIS, WHICH WAS INHABITED IN ANCIENT TIMES WELL BEYOND its present borders, is now host to several archaeological sites that are scattered throughout the surrounding desert in various stages of excavation. Among these are a few new sites recently opened for public viewing and exploration; some are only part of an extended complex of monuments where excavation has not yet begun or is just beginning. The first monument is the oldest structure yet found in Bahariya, dating to about 1295 B.C.; the next group of three—two tombs and a temple—date to the Twenty-sixth Dynasty, and the fifth monument is a Greek temple to Alexander the Great, the only one of its kind in Egypt.

TOMB OF AMENHOTEP HUY    At the site of Garet-Helwa, almost two miles south of Bahariya's ancient capital of El Qasr (now in El Bawiti), lies the tomb of Amenhotep Huy, governor of Bahariya. Georg Steindorff first discovered this New Kingdom site in 1900. It is the oldest known tomb found in the Oasis thus far, dating from the end of the Eighteenth Dynasty to the beginning of the Nineteenth, although since my team and I began to survey its outlying area in 1999, other tombs from earlier and later periods have started to surface. Because the Twelfth Dynasty kings of the Middle Kingdom paid attention to this strategically located settlement, it is highly possible that the area around the ancient capital will offer up some of the richest archaeology of the area.

This uniquely decorated rock-cut tomb suggests that Amenhotep Huy was well respected and the most powerful man in the Oasis at that time. The tomb is cut into a sandstone ridge, from which one can see the modern town of El Bawiti, and consists of an entrance hall with two columns and a second, four-columned room with three smaller burial chambers cut into the walls; two of these chambers have been divided into two tiny rooms. The architectural style is similar to that of Nile Valley tombs from the New Kingdom.

The reliefs in the Bahariya tomb are sunk rather than raised, and they are colored in traditional Egyptian style. Scenes in the hall with two columns depict the deceased performing the tasks he enjoyed the most. Banquet tables virtually overflow with flowers, bread, fruits, and cakes, and servants are shown gathering grapes, filling wine jars, and carrying sacks of corn, all part of the bountiful oasis harvest. Amenhotep Huy and his wife, Ourly, who was interred with her husband, are depicted worshiping Min, the god of fertility. The two columns cut out of the sandstone in the entrance hall, as well as the four in the main room, have long since crumbled and only their rectangular bases are visible. The main room is also decorated with scenes of daily life, such as an image of Amenhotep Huy and his wife praying to Osiris and Khonsu. Being buried in sand for thousands of years protected the colors, but they are now in worse condition than they were

The tomb of Amenhotep Huy, governor of the Oasis at the end of the Eighteenth Dynasty, the oldest one found at Bahariya to date

*Right:* Sunk reliefs in the tomb of Amenhotep Huy show the deceased praying to one of the gods in the underworld who sits in his chapel holding a knife to protect the tomb's owner.

*Below:* Two subsidiary burial chambers cut into the inscribed walls of the Tomb of Amenhotep Huy, where remains of mummies from the Roman Period were found, indicating that it was reused at a later period

*Page 182:* The mud-brick walls surrounding the Temple of Alexander the Great have yet to be fully excavated.

when Steindorff first described them. Unfortunately, the Oasis had no Antiquities Inspector, and they were never conserved properly after being uncovered, so we have lost most of the reliefs showing the deceased, as well as other religious scenes. Now all the monuments at Bahariya are being conserved.

Fortunately, the most important scenes are still decipherable in the burial chambers. The governor of Bahariya stands with a stick that conveys his authority and holds two sacks whose contents are not identified. Baskets of grain are being filled, probably to be sent to the Nile Valley, and the ceramic vessels appearing above the governor's head, which were once inscribed, are of the type used to hold beer and wine. We know that beer was produced in Bahariya; it was probably introduced by the Egyptians from the Nile Valley, where it was a main staple in pharaonic times. A hieroglyph written nearby, *Henkt,* refers to beer or the barley that was used to make it, so we can infer that the sacks being carried by Amenhotep Huy contained barley. Although we have no evidence, barley may have been produced in the Oasis and exported along with wine during the New Kingdom.

During the second excavation of Amenhotep Huy's tomb, in 1999, my team inspected the surrounding area and found another, larger tomb with about ten rectangular columns and the remains of several beautifully painted scenes. The name of the tomb's owner is not inscribed, but I believe that this tomb could be even older than that of Amenhotep Huy. Its burial chambers held ceramic vessels dated to the Late and Roman Periods, indicating that the tomb had been used during that time. Three chapels were also uncovered around Amenhotep's tomb, which could be part of a much larger temple. Systematic excavation of this site will provide us with a more complete picture spanning all eras of the Oasis.

## TOMB OF ZED-AMUN-EFANKH   As we have seen, Bahariya enjoyed a resurgence of power and prosperity in the Twenty-sixth Dynasty; one could even say it enjoyed a Golden Age during the reign of Ahmose II (570–526 B.C.), shortly before the Persian Empire occupied Egypt. To date, we have reopened three tombs that reflect the wealth of this era. The pharaohs and local leaders for whom these monuments were so reverently constructed represent some of the last of the native Egyptian rulers. My hope is that, even as we continue to unearth the more spectacular golden mummies of the prosperous Greco-Roman era, we can gain perspective about the redistribution of Egypt's power by studying earlier Oasis structures. I will provide here a brief description of the monuments as they exist today, including Fakhry's earlier observations, in an effort to initiate an ongoing study of the life of the Oasis just before the foreign occupation, a study that might identify the shifting conditions that led to the demise of traditional Egyptian culture.

The Tomb of Zed-Amun-efankh, a rock-cut chamber at the bottom of a shaft on the eastern ridge of El Bawiti, is unusual in that it was originally a single room with four rounded columns and seven false doors. (Other tombs of the period have square columns and a separate burial chamber.) The ceiling was painted with twelve vultures, the symbol of the goddess Nekhbet, surrounded by five- and six-sided stars. Having been plundered in antiquity, the tomb was robbed again at the turn of the twentieth century, when some mummies, beads, and amulets were taken. For

The burial chamber of Zed-Amun-efankh, a man of status in Bahariya Oasis during the Twenty-sixth Dynasty. The tomb is unique because he was interred in this main chamber surrounded by four columns carved from sandstone.

Right: A servant carries funerary furniture for use in the afterlife, while others praise the deceased in the Tomb of Zed-Amun-efankh.

those of us not so concerned with buried treasure, the tomb still contains a great deal of useful information. For example, Zed-Amun-efankh is not given any official titles in the tomb inscriptions, so we know he could not have held any governmental or priestly posts. Yet the surroundings in which he was buried, the wall paintings, and the great lengths to which the tomb builders went to give him privacy and security all attest to his having been a remarkably powerful man in the community. During the reign of Ahmose II, when Bahariya was a major exporter of wine and a crucial stop on the trade routes between sub-Saharan Africa, Egypt, and the coast of the Mediterranean, residents of the Oasis had an opportunity to make a sizeable fortune relatively quickly. These businessmen became the most powerful individuals of the Oasis at this time, just as powerful as the priests, if not more so. Therefore, we believe that Zed-Amun-efankh must have been a merchant or landowner, the only class that could have been able to afford a tomb like this one without having administrative or religious status. Clearly, it was no longer a matter of who was noble or pious enough to deserve such a "house of eternity," but who was wealthy enough to afford the builders and the materials. The same scenes and words previously reserved for god-kings, were, by the Late Period, used for the rich.

On the northern wall, to the right of the entrance, an inscription of the four sons of Horus reads: "An Offering that the king gives . . . to the Ka of the honored one under the Great God, to Osiris Zed-Amun-efankh, son of Weben-i'ah, true of voice. The honored one, his son, who stands behind him." A priest is pictured carrying red linen with which Zed-Amun-efankh was presumably mummified, as if he were royalty. Two gods—the sons of Horus, Duamutef and Qebehsenuef—run with knives "driving away the evil ones."

Invoked throughout the tomb is the god Osiris, king of the underworld, as Lord of the West, of the East, and of Abydos. Interestingly, images of Thoth, the god of wisdom, who was also associated with the moon, appear frequently in this tomb as well, and the hieroglyphs for the deceased's name repeatedly include the moon's symbol. These features contribute to other evidence that the moon deity warranted a special cult at Bahariya Oasis.

Scenes on the northern wall of the tomb show all four sons of Horus, and near them is a man offering a wooden box. All that remains of the scene on the western wall are four men and women raising their hands as if in a ritual gesture. The wife of Zed-Amun-efankh stands in a pose indicating praise; she wears a shawl with fringe, which is not entirely Egyptian in style, indicating that she may have been a foreigner.

The name of the deceased is inscribed on the cornices of each of the seven false doors. Six of the doors were cut into during the Roman Period to be used as additional adjoining burial chambers. Those who carried out this work took care not to damage inscriptions on the false doors, indicating that the workers were still respectful of the spirit of the deceased, or perhaps frightened by the consequences of their actions. By then, Egyptians must have seen no need to decorate or inscribe the walls, which were left with rough chisel marks.

**Below left:** During the Roman Period, niches were cut behind the false doors in the Tomb of Zed-Amun-efankh to be used as burial chambers. Wall paintings that depict the four sons of Horus carrying offerings have partially deteriorated.

**Below right:** The falcon-headed deity Duamutef, one of the four sons of Horus, holds a knife to protect the deceased in the underworld.

## TOMB OF BANNANTIU

Bannantiu is an uncommon name, meaning "the soul of those who have not." But Bannantiu, son of Zed-Amun-efankh, who was probably in the same business as his father, must also have been wealthy, because his tomb, situated next to his father's, is even bigger and more elaborately decorated. A square shaft cut into the sandstone leads down vertically about eighteen feet to a hall constructed like a Roman basilica, with two rows of columns dividing the long hall into three equal parts. Adjoining the hall are three smaller burial chambers. When Fakhry described this tomb, the traditional funerary scenes painted on the walls were beautifully preserved, but today, because of erosion and weathering, we are left with only partial scenes, although the colors are still vivid. One column lost most of its decoration when a section of it was stolen in 1979. Now, finally, the tomb is undergoing thorough conservation for the first time.

When you first enter the tomb down a recently installed metal stairway that resembles a fire escape, you can see, directly to the right of the entrance, the painted image of Bannantiu with a shaved head standing behind Anubis, who introduces him to Amun and Horus. Amun appears as Kamutef, the "bull of [Amun's] mother." The deceased's name is written *Bannantiu-Zed-efankh*, although it seems that the artist made a mistake and omitted the name *Amun*, for it should read *Bannantiu-Zed-Amun-efankh*.

In front of the jackal-headed Anubis are three hieroglyphic lines with the god's name and title, which translate as "words spoken by Anubis, Lord of the Cemetery, the great god Lord of Hetret" (a place in heaven). Amun is depicted leaning on a column shaped like a tree with palm fronds and holding a stick with three animal skins. In front of the god is an inscription that translates as "words spoken by the god Amun-Ra, the bull of his mother." Next to Horus are statues

of six gods standing on sacred pillars, including the jackal-god Wepwawet, opener of the way into the underworld. Like a wealthy man of today, whose funeral is attended by all of the world's dignitaries and celebrities, Bannantiu is assisted in his passage by all the most important deities.

At the Feast of Nefer-tem, which is pictured on the western wall, six symbols of minor gods, including Khonsu, a god of the moon, are mounted on stands. Two mourning goddesses, Isis and Nephtys, stand at either end of the mummification table, as Anubis holds a vessel over the face of the deceased, beneath whose head stand four canopic jars and the sign for the sky at (see page 136). Bannantiu, pictured as a mummy, holds symbols that signify his rebirth. On the other side of the entrance is Osiris, represented as the living king, with his wife and sister, Isis, who holds in her right hand the sign of life and in her left hand the ankh. On the columns are scenes of Geb, god of the earth, and Nut, goddess of the sky.

Tomb paintings show the solar boat delivering the deceased to the underworld. Nefer-tem, god of the morning, is seated in the bow of the boat and is depicted as a child with his finger in his mouth, signifying the new day.

The south wall shows Shu, god of the air and sunlight, lifting the sun disk, in the middle of which Khonsu is pictured putting a finger of his left hand into his mouth and holding a scepter, symbol of rebirth, in his right. The eight gods from the ancient creative myth of Ashmonein (a site in Middle Egypt) are shown with heads in the form of snakes and frogs. Around the entrance to the burial chamber are scenes representing the *Hours of Dwat* (*dwat* refers to the underworld) from *The Book of the Dead* and the night boat of the sun-god (the solar boat), in which the deceased is carried through the underworld. In the bow sits the god Nefer-tem, son of the sun-god Atem, with a finger in his mouth to represent Bannantiu as a child going forth into new life. Nefer-tem's other hand holds two scepters, which symbolize sovereignty and rebirth. Also in the boat are Horakhty and Sekhmet, as well as a baboon holding an offering. Behind the sun disk is Heka, the god of magic. Three jackals pull the solar boat with ropes, followed by more goddesses. A scene on the north wall shows the deceased worshiping Horus, as the gods Khepri and Heka and the goddess Sekhmet stand nearby; above them is the sun disk, on which Aten is depicted wearing a double crown.

Of the three smaller rooms off the main hall, the north and south rooms were never completed. They were apparently reused at a later date, because they contain two sarcophagi dating to the Roman Period. The western room—the original burial chamber—is full of beautiful scenes that were painted over a layer of polished plaster. The two most important scenes in Bannantiu's burial chamber show him standing before the gods in the Hall of Judgment, having been accepted for eternal life. His financial status, in spite of the lack of religious or political credentials, earned him special treatment and entry into the afterlife.

Osiris sits in judgment on a chair in his mummified form before an offering table that holds many items, such as food and sacred incense. Isis, Thoth, Horus, Seth, and Taweret are all present for the weighing of Bannantiu's heart against the feather of Maat, who presents the deceased to Osiris. In the next scene Osiris receives Bannantiu for his passage into the underworld, witnessed by Isis, Hathor, Anubis, Horus, Nephtys, and another Anubis. There is nothing unusual in the way these burial chamber scenes are rendered; what is striking is simply that a merchant could purchase himself such preferential treatment by the gods.

Ahmed Fakhry, whose interpretation of the scenes was somewhat different, observed that the worship of the moon-god was a priority in Bahariya and other oasis communities, including Kharga and Dakhla, where the moon's rhythms rather than the Nile floods played an important role in helping residents keep track of time and dates. They must have relied heavily on its light and its position in the sky for traveling by night, when the sun made it almost impossible to travel through the desert by day. It is easy to see why the moon rather than the sun, which posed a threat in the middle of a seemingly endless arid desert, would have been for Bahariya a symbol of sustained life.

Fakhry noted that certain gods whose importance seemed to wane at certain times or in certain regions would sometimes return to their former significance. Khonsu, one of the earliest Egyptian gods whose image was carved on temple walls accompanying pharaohs on ceremonial occasions as early as the First Dynasty, appears again in funerary scenes in Bahariya during the

In the tomb of Bannantiu the vividly painted wall scenes in the hall with four square-pillars and the adjoining burial chamber were recently restored and preserved by conservators.

Bannantiu is shown standing with his hand raised and accompanied by the sun-god Ra in the center with the lioness-goddess Sekhmet, on the solar boat journeying through the night to the underworld.

New Kingdom and the Late Period. The goddess of inundation, Mert, also makes a reappearance in Oasis tombs, perhaps because she is associated with water, on which the Oasis dwellers, of course, depended for their very lives. Another unusual reference to a much earlier period is the appearance in Bannantiu's tomb of a baboon deity in a scene with the eight gods of Ashmonein (which Fakhry called by the Greek name Hermopolis), which is also seen in the tombs of Ped-Ashtar and Thaty (see chapter 15). Ha, god of the Western Desert, first mentioned in *The Pyramid Texts* but thereafter appearing only infrequently in Old Kingdom tombs and *The Book of the Dead*, was featured prominently among the principal deities in Oasis tombs and on the Temple of Ain el-Muftella.

TEMPLE OF AIN EL-MUFTELLA  The monuments in the site of Ain el-Muftella were built around a spring near El Qasr, the capital of Bahariya during the Twenty-sixth Dynasty; indeed, the temple may have served as the town center. As described by Fakhry in 1939, the temple appeared to be four separate chapels, and so he called them the chapels of Ain el-Muftella, but when we examined the structure in 1977, we realized that there is actually only one temple. It is possible that some parts of the temple and surrounding buildings were established as early as the New Kingdom and then refurbished during the Twenty-sixth Dynasty, added onto by the Greeks, and finally completed much later by the Romans.

At least a few sections of this temple were built by the high priest Zed-Khonsu-efankh during the reign of Ahmose II of the Twenty-sixth Dynasty. The priest's brother, Sheben-Khonsu, was governor of the town, which flourished until the Roman Period. Zed-Khonsu-efankh succeeded his brother and then had another chapel added to those he had already built. After excavating the area, Fakhry realized that it would not be preserved if it were exposed to the elements and the public, so he reburied it in sand. We restored its original structure and preserved the remaining scenes, so that both visitors and archaeologists can appreciate all the beauty and wisdom it has to offer.

Four stone chapels decorated with painted sunk reliefs make up the center of the building. The scenes are similar to those found in other temples built in Upper Egypt at this time. The first chapel has two large halls, which once had vaulted ceilings painted with geometrical designs of intersecting lines, and the halls were adjoined by one smaller room on each side. Most of the reliefs portray Ahmose II wearing his crown of Upper and Lower Egypt, standing beside Governor Zed-Khonsu-efankh as they make their offerings to thirteen gods: Mahesa, Bastet, Amun, Mut, Khonsu, Harsaphis, Hathor, Thoth, Nehem-awa, Amun with a ram's head, Mut, Anubis, and Isis. Sheben-Khonsu is sometimes shown standing next to his brother, and in a few cases the god Ha is included also in the procession. Nehem-awa as the consort of Thoth had a prominent place in Oasis worship.

In the scenes located at the side entrance, Ahmose II stands with the ankh in his right hand. Next to him are the hippopotamus-goddess Taweret, Horus with a crown and sun disk, and Hathor; behind them is a scene in which a child puts his finger into his mouth, a naked god, a goddess whose name is not inscribed, and the goddess Maat with her distinctive feather. All of these figures are facing the gods Montu, Horus, and Sekhmet, the lioness-goddess. A few ancient artifacts were found in this particular chapel, including a statue of the goddess Bastet, a stone emblem of a head of Hathor, a statuette of a king, one of Thoth, and fragments of a bronze vase.

The second chapel was also built by Zed-Khonsu-efankh, who is pictured with a shaved head praying before Osiris and, as in the first temple, making offerings to a procession of deities (here with the addition of Seshat, the goddess of writing), alongside his brother as governor and Ahmose II. There are scenes showing the symbolic mourning of Osiris by his sisters, and one

Archaeologists covered the largest of the chapels of Ain el-Muftella, constructed by Ahmose II near the end of the Twenty-sixth Dynasty, with a wooden ceiling to protect the ancient site.

Well-preserved wall carvings of gods and goddesses in a chapel at Ain el-Muftella. Sandstone rocks, once used in the chapel, were replaced above the wall inscriptions during conservation.

*Below:* Ahmose II presents offerings to a god and goddess in one of the chapels at Ain el-Muftella.

scene contains inscriptions of the names of various deities. To the right of the entrance a priest can be seen standing with offerings to Osiris. In the second scene on this wall the pharaoh stands facing the god Thoth, while scenes on the west wall show him making offerings, followed by Osiris, who stands in mummified position.

The third chapel is a large room with two opposing entrances built of dolerite and sandstone blocks. This was apparently a center of worship for the god Bes, as one wall is devoted to a large figure of the deity, of which only the bottom half is still visible. The fourth chapel, also built by the priest Zed-Khonsu-efankh, is made of brick and stone and does not seem to have been painted, although there is a carved relief of Ahmose II in the presence of Khnum and Horus.

Artifacts found more recently at the site include a faience statuette less than three inches high of Isis holding Horus in her lap and another of Sekhmet with the sun disk behind her for protection. These objects may have been worn as necklaces. Two small scarabs were also discovered; on the bottom of one a man holds a stick as if in war or defense. Other small items include Seth with a donkey's head and a *wedjat*-eye amulet.

After Ahmed Fakhry concluded his excavation, he wrote: "There is no doubt that the tombs of the other members of the family are still buried, either under the houses of El Bawiti or in one of the ridges surrounding it. It would be a good thing to find one day the Tomb of Zed-Khonsu-efankh." If the three tombs of this man's relatives are any reflection of the wealth of his family, and if his tomb has not yet been plundered, then it will surely be a spectacular discovery. I believe we are close.

## THE TEMPLE OF ALEXANDER THE GREAT
Bahariya Oasis has the honor of being home to the only known temple in all Egypt dedicated to Alexander the Great, yet it was purely by accident that Ahmed Fakhry first came across its scattered remains while he was searching for a stela of Thutmose II that he never found. In 1938 he was exploring a spring called Ain el-Tabinieh in a neighborhood mentioned by Sir John Gardner Wilkinson in 1837. On his last day in Bahariya, Fakhry found himself standing on a mound of sand surrounded by stones that he thought might have been a New Kingdom temple. He made a note of the mound but had to leave the site, as his funds were nearly depleted. It was not until 1942 that he had enough resources to return and complete the excavation, and it was then that he discovered the sandstone blocks on which were carved the cartouches of Alexander the Great.

The Temple of Alexander the Great near the Valley of the Golden Mummies, the only temple in Egypt dedicated to the Macedonian king. Alexander ushered in the Greco-Roman Period when he usurped power from the Persian rulers in 332 B.C.

**The long corridor that led worshipers in Greco-Roman times past several side rooms to the main sanctuary**

When Alexander came to the Egyptian border in October of 332 B.C., he and his army of soldiers camped at El Farama in Sinai, which was protected by a small Egyptian garrison. The Persian king of Egypt had very few soldiers left to defend himself after Egyptian forces had mounted a revolution against him, so he surrendered to Alexander's army. Alexander went with his army to Memphis, where he made an offering to the sacred bull of Apis and crowned himself king in a festival that shared Egyptian and Greek elements. Egypt celebrated him as their liberator.

Herodotus relates that Alexander then went to the island of Pharos and chose the site of an ancient settlement called Raqote as the place for a new city to be built in the Greek style as the center of Greek and Egyptian culture—what is now the city of Alexandria. Alexander then journeyed to Siwa Oasis to meet with the oracle of Amun. Of all Alexander's notable accomplishments, I find this to be the most fascinating—to bring his army all the way through the desert with little water in order to pay respect to Amun and consult a spiritual wise man. I imagine he must have embarked on this difficult journey to emulate Hercules or another Greek god hero.

It has been said that the priest of Amun gave Alexander permission only to enter the sanctuary in his everyday clothing and that when they sat together the priest greeted the conqueror as his son. Alexander did not understand at first but was advised that he had just been accepted as the son of the god Amun, and he said: "I accept this title, my father." Having thus received divine kingship from Amun, the Macedonian could be considered the rightful pharaoh of Egypt. As Aristotle's former pupil, Alexander was clever enough to realize that the ancient gods meant everything to the Egyptians and that nothing had offended them more than the Persians' slaying of the Apis bull. Wisely, Alexander chose to respect the Egyptians' gods, rituals, and festivals. In this way, he not only won sovereignty over the Egyptians, he also won their hearts. So began the Ptolemaic Period.

I am convinced that Alexander the Great did not return to Alexandria from Siwa by the same route through Mersy-Matrouh but rather took a shortcut through the desert, along the same road that exists today, stopping on the way in Bahariya Oasis. If he touched the ground of Bahariya, it would have been an appropriate place for a temple to be built in his honor; there is no other acceptable explanation for his temple's having been located there. Because the Oasis prospered during the reign of Alexander the Great and had a considerable Greek population, we estimate that he would have been given a great reception. In any case, Alexander or possibly one of his followers may have come back to the Oasis and constructed an elaborate temple in his honor. I first visited the site in 1977 and came back to reexcavate it from 1993 to 1994, including several rooms that had never been cleared before.

One of the largest temples in the Oasis, the Temple of Alexander the Great consists of at least forty-five chambers. It is situated about three miles west of El Qasr and opens from the south through a gate. The temple is built of mud brick encased in sandstone. It sits on a hilltop overlooking the Valley of the Golden Mummies, which is only three hundred yards away. In front and around it are separate storage rooms and houses, possibly used by the temple guards and priests. On the east side is a building that could have been used for administrative purposes; only two chambers were roofed with large limestone blocks, marked with Greek graffiti that have since disappeared. More rooms were still being added when the construction was left unfinished.

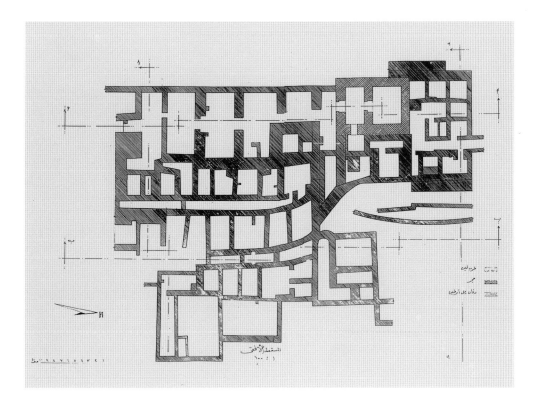

Plan of the Temple of Alexander the Great

To the right of the entrance is a carved relief in which one can see only the lower half of two people facing each other. This could be Alexander depicted not as a conqueror but as a divinely decreed pharaoh making offerings to the principal deities. On the north wall of the second room are two scenes divided into upper and lower sections. Although the upper section is damaged, the lower was covered by temple debris, which preserved its color. Alexander is offering two vessels, perhaps cups of Oasis wine, to Horus and Isis, who each hold a scepter in one hand and the ankh in the other. Behind Alexander stands a priest wearing a long white robe and holding incense and some type of tool. They stand before an offering table laden with bread, meat, cucumbers, pomegranates and other fruits, as well as vessels for ointments.

In another scene the pharaoh presents an offering of incense to the god Amun, and behind him are the governor and the first priest of the Oasis, who also hold offerings of incense. There are still visible some faded remains of an offering table full of bread, meat, vegetables, liquor, and flowers, beside which appears Amun followed by goddesses, one of which may be his wife, Mut. On one of the blocks discovered in the debris were inscribed the two names of Alexander the Great inside two cartouches: his throne name, Setp n Ra Mery Amun, and his given name, Alexander. Although they no longer exist, other inscriptions described by Fakhry document the fact that the temple was built during the reign of Alexander the Great to honor the principal deities Amun and Horus.

A large altar made of red granite, a material not indigenous to any of the oases, was found outside the temple. It must have been transported all the way from the Nile Valley. When one considers this journey, presumably by donkey, one cannot help but be impressed with the Egyptians' tenacity and dedication to their spiritual practices. Perhaps the altar was later dragged outside and left when Christians under Emperor Justinian systematically closed what he considered to be pagan temples.

Artifacts found inside the temple include Greek, Roman, and Coptic pottery shards, and painted vases, fragments of bronze statues, and amulets from the Ptolemaic Period. In the

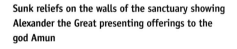

**Sunk reliefs on the walls of the sanctuary showing Alexander the Great presenting offerings to the god Amun**

Alexander the Great is shown presenting offerings to the god Amun, one of the favored deities of the Oasis during the Greco-Roman Period, to whom the temple is dedicated.

temple corridor, we found a small statue of the priest of Ra and around the temple, coins from the fifth and sixth centuries A.D. Semitic pottery from Asia covered with rectangular marks and human figures, as well as pottery shards and lamps from the Coptic Period and later, seems to indicate that the Christians inhabited the temple until the twelfth century. Some of the chambers show signs of reuse as dwelling places until as late as the Middle Ages.

We also discovered a bronze statue that we believe portrays the wife of Alexander the Great, because she is depicted as a royal figure. A stone inscribed with the image of the winged sun disk may have been a part of the temple entrance. We are still excavating the extended outer wall and therefore expect to find more. Perhaps some evidence could still surface proving that Alexander the Great himself visited Bahariya.

In 323 B.C., after being mummified in Babylon using Egyptian techniques, Alexander the

Great was placed in a gold coffin and transported in a grand procession to Greece to be buried. As a king of Macedonian origin, he would have been given a traditional burial in Aegae, but his successor, Ptolemy, had him taken instead to Egypt to be interred in Alexandria, the capital city named after him. It is in this coastal necropolis, which he had planned and loved, that his mummified body lay throughout the reign of the Ptolemies, until the city was sacked by the Romans. The exact location of Alexander's tomb has not been known since that time, when political power in Egypt changed hands and the city was rebuilt. Some scholars believe his body may still rest beneath the Nebi Daniel Mosque in Alexandria, but because the mosque is at risk of being undermined, an extensive excavation of the subterranean caverns is impossible.

Because the whereabouts of Alexander's tomb has never been confirmed and continues to

The author examines pottery shards found in the Temple of Alexander the Great in order to determine how long the temple continued to be used after the Roman Period.

be the subject of much speculation, I have already received inquiries into the possibility of his having been buried in Bahariya. Despite this being the only existing temple of Alexander the Great in Egypt, there is no reason to believe he would have been buried, or even reburied, there. Legend has it that Alexander once asked to be buried at Siwa Oasis, where he had been declared a god, and in 1995 a Greek archaeologist claimed that she had discovered his tomb, with inscriptions establishing that his body lay in Siwa. Her theory was subsequently disproved, when it was found that her alleged evidence did not contain any reference to Alexander. No funerary temple or sacred burial site exists for Alexander at the site of his temple. Nevertheless, I believe that the people of Bahariya were buried in the area nearby, now known as the Valley of the Golden Mummies, because they wanted to be close to this legendary god-king throughout eternity.

# REDISCOVERED
# TOMBS

THE SANDSTONE WALLS CRUMBLED AT MY TOUCH, AS I CROUCHED DOWN TO crawl through a passage into the first burial chamber of Ta-Nefret-Bastet, one of a group of Twenty-sixth Dynasty tombs that we had uncovered in a residential area just outside El Bawiti. Roman mummies were stashed in side rooms and were now blackened from resin, the linen flaking away from their bodies like ash to reveal their bones. These cavernous underground chambers cut out of the rock in about 500 B.C. seemed to have been made roughly, perhaps hurriedly, without a precise plan. Because we were still in the first stages of excavation, I had to step gingerly over Roman sarcophagus lids left lying on the floor by grave robbers, in order to move through the three adjoining burial chambers. That day in October 1999 was no different from any other day of digging. I had arrived at the site earlier than usual, while the air was still cool, in order to assess what needed to be done that day, and I noticed a space under one of the walls that I had not seen before. My heart started to race.

When Fakhry found these three tombs in 1947, he was eager to move on, hoping to explore as much ground as he could in a short time. So he described the tombs only briefly and left them unexcavated. At that time, a revolution was brewing (one that would result in Egypt's becoming a democratic republic), and the rules pertaining to antiquities changed as quickly as government bureaucrats, so that archaeological research foundered. The desert's shifting sand reburied several sites, as it had done repeatedly during political transitions for thousands of years. New people filled positions without knowing what excavation work had been in progress, and important sites were forgotten.

Because of these conditions, I realized that there might very likely be more to this particular set of tombs than we had originally suspected on the basis of the reports filed by Fakhry fifty years earlier. It was apparent from the substantial space beneath the wall I was looking at that it was not made of solid rock. We had already excavated everything Fakhry had referred to in his work on Bahariya Oasis, so I concluded that there must be another, undiscovered room on the far side of the wall. If so, it would be one that had not been investigated since antiquity—perhaps, if I was lucky again, an intact tomb.

It is amazing that unknown ancient tombs can still exist in such populated areas, but it is not hard to understand why. No Antiquities Inspectorate had stayed on this site in El Bawiti after Fakhry left in 1950, so the people of the village quickly built homes right on top of the three tombs, perhaps hoping to unearth their own treasures and sell them to support their families during a very difficult economic time. These buildings went up over the ancient site without consequence, since no antiquities laws existed to protect monuments until 1951 and even

An unfinished Roman limestone sarcophagus in the burial chamber of Thaty, which was reused in Roman times

*Page 202:* A hole in the western wall of the newly discovered tomb, probably made by the Romans who later reused the burial site and left behind several unfinished sarcophagi in the corridor beyond the hole

after that, no inspectors were on site to enforce them. The tombs had been hidden ever since.

Even when I became Inspector of Bahariya in 1977, I had never heard of the tombs. I knew the site only as the location of a mud-brick cenotaph built in 1950, a symbolic tomb of Sheikh Soby, a Muslim Sufi who was much beloved, like a saint, for his miracles. Locals still make pilgrimages to the area to leave offerings at the tomb and to touch the ground.

In September 1999, everything was quiet as usual in El Bawiti, when a resident told Ashry Shaker that five local young men were planning to get married. They each needed a house but had no money, so someone in the village suggested that if they dug under the homes near the cenotaph, they might be able to find artifacts they could sell for "marriage money." Ashry Shaker rewarded the man who came to him with this information and then promptly related it to me. I told him to have one of his inspectors hide behind the houses to catch the boys when they dug into the earth near the cenotaph. Every night for two weeks, Shaker and his assistant waited there, but the boys, who must have been alerted, never showed up. So we began to excavate the area ourselves. About twenty feet down we found the three tombs Fakhry had mentioned: the tombs of Ped-Ashtar, Thaty, and Ta-Nefret-Bastet. Pottery shards were strewn around as if they had been handled, but it seemed unlikely that the families who had built houses above the ancient site had derived much benefit from their location. The tombs showed evidence of having already been

robbed and reused in Roman times, and any remaining artifacts would have been of little value. Fakhry himself recovered only seventeen small amulets, including two headrests. It was very lucky the boys didn't make their way into the tombs, not because there was nothing of value for them but because if they had been caught, they would not be living in new marriage houses now. They would have been put in jail for more than five years. In any case, we are fortunate that this incident in 1999 led us to rediscover the site. Even in 1947, when Fakhry recorded his findings in detail, the three Twenty-sixth Dynasty tombs were in less than pristine condition. Since then, water from the homes has damaged painted scenes on the walls, so much of what we know comes from Fakhry's reports rather than from the appearance of the paintings themselves.

## TOMB OF PED-ASHTAR

This set of three adjoining tombs is entered by climbing down a shaft into a cavelike maze of rooms with rounded walls. The first tomb belongs to a man named Ped-Ashtar, who lived during or just before the reign of King Apries (589–570 B.C.). He was the grandfather of Zed-Khonsu-efankh, the governor of Bahariya, whose tomb is probably nearby, although we have not yet found it. Ped-Ashtar was a high priest of Khonsu and a priest of Horus, as was his father, Harkheb. The unusual name, Ped-Ashtar, means "the gift of Ashtar," a Syrian goddess whose reference here is indicative of the merging iconography in the Oasis between Egyptian and invading cultures of the Third Intermediate and Late Periods.

This is the oldest tomb in Bahariya after that of Amenhotep Huy. Its three chambers, the hall with four columns, and the vaulted ceilings were once painted with scenes representing the hours of day and night and the forty-two gods of the Hall of Judgment. We know from Fakhry's descriptions that some of the images differed from earlier standard tomb scenes. These alterations give us insight into how the religious practices may have been changing at the time the tomb was decorated.

Earlier versions of *The Book of the Dead*, for example, give the number of the Souls of Pe and Souls of Nekhen as three each (Pe and Nekhen were two towns in Middle Egypt). The Tomb of

The god Anubis, lord of the cemetery, presents offerings to the deceased in the Tomb of Ped-Ashtar.

**The wife of Ped-Ashtar in his Twenty-sixth Dynasty tomb stands in the presence of Horus.**

Ped-Ashtar showed only two souls for each god, while in the Tomb of Thaty, next to this one, there were four. In the Late Period, the names of the Souls of Pe and Nekhen were the same as those of the four sons of Horus, which is unusual. Another unique feature of this tomb was the way in which the names of the eight gods of Ashmonein were inscribed: Amun and Amaunet were replaced by Nun and Naunet. In pharaonic Egypt, Osiris was most often mourned by his wife and sister, Isis, and by Nephtys. In many of Bahariya's tombs, these traditional goddesses were replaced with Mert and Wadjyt at the head and foot of Osiris's sarcophagus.

The only other apparent addition to an otherwise typical scene of Maat introducing Ped-Ashtar to Osiris was the depiction of siphons, or long tubes, leading from one vessel on a table to a vessel below. Historians believe this unique invention was brought to Egypt by the Syrians during the Eighteenth Dynasty, because there are no other instances in which this type of device is shown before that time.

TOMB OF THATY   Connected to Ped-Ashtar's tomb by a break in its northern wall is the tomb of Thaty, grandson of Ped-Ashtar, son of Pedisi. The hall with columns and the two chambers contained typical inscriptions of Thaty's titles and parentage, offerings to Osiris, scenes from the Hall of Judgment, the journey of the solar boat, and the journey of the moon. Thaty's family lineage was lovingly invoked and honored in the inscribed text, which read like a kind of family tree of priests: "Thaty, the priest of Khonsu, the repeater priest of Amun-Horu-Khonsu, Thaty, son of the same man Pedisi, son of the same man Ped-Ashtar, son of the same man Harkheb, born of N'as."

In one scene, Thaty's wife, Ta-Nefret-Bastet and his daughter were shown raising their arms in prayer for the deceased; both women are wearing a unique style of dress. Egyptian women in the Old Kingdom always wore a plain white linen dress with one breast bared. By the New Kingdom, dresses were close-fitting with multicolored patterns, and they covered both breasts. Here, and in the tomb of Zed-Amun-efankh, however, each wife wore a robe of non-Egyptian origin with fringed edges and a scarf around the neck, with one end falling over one breast, the other down the back. A few of the women wore sleeveless cloaks.

Although some fringed robes can be seen in earlier processions of Libyan women, this variation is found nowhere else except in Phoenician and early Greek civilization. Therefore, we can conclude that this wealthy family of priests and governors of Bahariya had married into families of some newly arrived foreigners, probably Greeks, who were the leading merchants in the world at that time. The use of this fringe-style dress became more common in the Nile Valley during the Late Period as Greek culture gradually made its influence felt on traditional Egyptian ways of life.

Fakhry also found eight sarcophagi in two chambers reused for Roman burials and then robbed in modern times. The sarcophagi would have been lowered down a sand ramp through a side tunnel, which was then refilled. There is a hole in the wall leading to the tomb of Ped-Ashtar, where thieves hammered through a false door. One can still see typical scenes of mummification by Anubis, although the plaster is flaking off the wall. The purification of the deceased takes place

A detail of the mural below showing female deities carrying the deceased

*Below:* In the adjoining Tomb of Thaty, grandson of Ped-Ashtar, the lion-headed god Amun-Min, seen standing with an erection to symbolize fertility and rebirth, is followed by a procession of female deities carrying a mummy for delivery to the afterlife.

before Thoth, who appears in the form of a baboon, and Isis is seen nursing her child Horus. In mummified form, the deceased is drawn with an erection, which signifies his resurrection into the afterlife. The only artifacts left behind were a few Osirian statuettes made of faience and two canopic jar lids topped with heads of Anubis.

## TOMB OF TA-NEFRET-BASTET

Ta-Nefret-Bastet was Thaty's wife, "daughter of Pedisi, born of N'as," according to the inscriptions on the tomb as recorded by Fakhry. She was depicted in her own burial chamber wearing the same unusual fringed clothes that she wore in her husband's. Although the black Egyptian headdress was traditional, the portrait showed pink skin and black eyes, further evidence that she may have been the descendant of a Phoenician or Greek family. Her tomb, which was built very close to and behind Thaty's, was left unfinished. We do not know why she was buried in a separate tomb.

The only remaining wall painting in the Twenty-sixth Dynasty tomb of Ta Nefret-Bastet, wife of Thaty, where plaster crumbles easily off the soft sandstone. Ta Nefret-Bastet, pictured in a white robe, is being led by the goddess Isis into the presence of Osiris, who is followed by Nephtys.

*Below:* Unfinished limestone sarchophagi were placed during Roman times in the corridors between the tombs of Ped-Ashtar and Ta Nefret-Bastet.

It was in the tomb of Ta-Nefret-Bastet that I approached the opening under a wall that morning in October 1999. I considered waiting until some of our workers could carefully dig out a larger entrance for me to fit through safely, but my curiosity outweighed my reason. I got down on my belly and tried to peek underneath, but the wall was too thick to see what was on the other side. I decided to take my chances and climb under the wall but to play it safe by taking along my assistant Mohammed Tiyab, who was in charge of the excavation.

The opening was about one-and-a-half feet high. I managed to squeeze through by wriggling through the red sandstone like a snake. When my feet were clear of the hole, I tried to stand up but realized that the space was only about three to five feet high. When we held up the light, the first thing we saw was each other—red hair, red clothes, red faces; we were covered in red sandstone. We laughed at each other. I love this part of the adventure of archaeology.

The space appeared to be about ten feet long. Its ceiling was vaulted and painted with still-colorful scenes of gods and goddesses from *The Book of the Dead.* We were very excited, because this meant we were entering into yet another tomb, one that showed no signs of water damage or vandalism. I looked around and noticed a hole in the western wall. Fakhry could not have known about this tomb, or his notes would have mentioned it, so I assume that part of the sandstone

Painted sunk relief of Nekhbet, the vulture goddess, whose outstretched wings over the entrance to a newly discovered burial chamber protect the deceased within

must have crumbled away naturally since 1950. I brought my lamp closer to inspect the hole, which was about one foot square, just large enough to put my light into. Mohammed was nearby, trying to peer into the hole at the same time, which was impossible. He kept asking me: "What do you see, doctor? What do you see?"

I found myself saying the same words that Howard Carter had said to Lord Carnarvon: "Wonderful things . . . wonderful things." When I looked at Mohammed and saw how anxious he was, as if he were going to burst if he didn't get a look, I told him to wait while I described everything in detail. This second room in the fourth tomb was about twenty feet long and six feet wide and it contained a large stone sarcophagus with a rounded lid. Unlike the situation in the other three tombs, this lid was still on top of the sarcophagus, not on the floor, which indicated that it was intact! This was obviously an undisturbed burial chamber containing a large anthropoid coffin surrounded by pottery and artifacts that I could not recognize because they were buried under the sand. My mind was reeling. Who does the tomb belong to? How many more rooms lie waiting for us beyond these two? Will they provide us with a good look into history? Is it possible that their mummies and funerary objects are still undisturbed?

It is these moments, when it is crucially important to stay calm, that I find extremely difficult. I stayed there for an hour wondering what I should do, because it appeared as if the chamber's entrance led to an area where some modern dwellings were situated. I decided to leave and return the following day to survey further.

I took Ashry Shaker with me to figure out how we could enter the new tomb, and we concluded that the only way to enter the second chamber was to demolish ten of the twenty houses above ground. We arranged a meeting with the owners of the houses. The residents there are very poor and very kind. In the course of our discussions, we realized that they actually had no legal right to the land, or any legal document to prove that they owned the houses. Therefore, by law, the government could not give them any compensation. I asked Ashry to record the names of all the residents and the sizes of each house. Then I wrote a report to the Antiquities Department explaining the situation and asked them to issue a decree to demolish the homes under the protection of the police. I met with the mayor of Bahariya the next day to see how we could help these people. We decided to give them each a piece of land, although we could not pay them any money. When I explained our decision to the home owners, I thought they would refuse, but they were actually very happy. I was surprised at this and asked Ashry the reason. He smiled and said most of them had other houses in town. One requirement we made clear to the authorities in charge of the demolition was that the cenotaph of Sheikh Soby must stay in its present location, because his spirit may help us in the discovery of something incredible.

I firmly believe that these tombs will prove very important to the history of Bahariya. My team of archaeologists is eagerly awaiting the opportunity to move ahead with the excavations there. Like a child sitting before a pile of wrapped gifts, I can hardly wait until we enter this untouched tomb of the Twenty-sixth Dynasty and continue our excavation at the Valley of the Golden Mummies. I plan to document these further excavations in the second edition of this book.

What else lies beyond these walls? What kinds of mummies lie in the tombs that we have yet to discover? We will have to wait until the next digging season to find out, but I expect nothing less than spectacular results. It is even possible that we may find mummies of the upper class and of Roman officials that are even more lavishly decorated than the golden mummies. This is why I love my job: There is always so much more to uncover and each day is full of surprises. Now I feel there was a reason, after all, that I moved from the site at the Giza Pyramids to Bahariya Oasis. I can only call it destiny.

The cenotaph of Sheikh Soby, an Islamic monument where local villagers come to pray for him to answer their wishes, near the site of the Twenty-sixth Dynasty tombs

# CHRONOLOGY OF ANCIENT EGYPT

**Predynastic Period: c. 5500–3100** B.C.

Neolithic period: farming and domestication of animals and first settlements. Simple pottery; copper and gold working. Local rulers

**Early Dynastic Period: c. 3100–2686** B.C.

(Dynasties 1 and 2)

Unification under one ruler (Narmer); capital at Memphis and royal tombs at Abydos and Saqqara

**Old Kingdom: c. 2686–2181** B.C.

Dynasty 3 (c. 2686–2613)
   Sanakht           Step Pyramid at Saqqara
   Djoser
   Sekhemkhet
   Khaba
   Huni

Dynasty 4 (c. 2613–2494)    Pyramids at Giza
   Sneferu
   Khufu
   Djedefra
   Khafra
   Menkaura
   Shepseskaf

Dynasty 5 (c. 2465–2325)    Pyramids and Sun Temples
   Userkaf           at Abu Sir and Saqqara;
   Sahura           *Pyramid Texts*
   Neferirkara
   Shepseskara
   Raneferef
   Nyuserra
   Menkauhor
   Djedkara
   Unas

Dynasty 6 (c. 2325–2150)    Strong beginning but
   Teti            decline during long reign
   Userkara        of Pepy II; pyramids at
   Pepy I           Saqqara
   Merenra
   Pepy II
   Nitiqret

**First Intermediate Period: c. 2181–2055** B.C.

Dynasties 7–10

Collapse of central government; country divided among local rulers; famine and poverty

**Middle Kingdom: c. 2055–1650** B.C.

Dynasty 11 (2055–1985)    Reunification of Egypt by
   Mentuhotep II     Theban rulers
   Mentuhotep III
   Mentuhotep IV

Dynasty 12 (1985–1795)    Powerful central govern-
   Amenemhat I      ment; capital at Lisht
   Senrusret I
   Amenemhat II
   Senrusret II
   Senrusret III
   Amenemhat III
   Amenemhat IV
   Sobekneferu

Dynasty 13 (1795–after 1650)   Rapid succession of rulers; country in decline

**Second Intermediate Period: c. 1650–1550** B.C.

Dynasty 14 (1750–1650)    Series of minor rulers
Dynasty 15, 16           Asiatic princes ruling in the Delta

Dynasty 17 (1650–1550)    Theban dynasty begins
   Intef            reunification
   Taa I (Senakhtenra)
   Taa II (Seqenenra)
   Kamose

**New Kingdom: c. 1550–1069** B.C.

Dynasty 18 (1550–1295)    Reunification and expul-
   Ahmose          sion of Asiatics in north;
   Amenhotep I      period of greatest expan-
   Thutmose I        sion; Thebes (Luxor)
   Thutmose II       becomes main residence
   Thutmose III
   Hatshepsut
   Amenhotep II
   Thutmose IV
   Amenhotep III

Amenhotep IV (Akhenaten)
Tutankhamun
Ay
Horemheb
Dynasty 19 (1295–1186)     After glorious reign of
    Ramses I              Ramses II, prosperity
    Sety I                threatened by invasions of
    Ramses II           Sea Peoples in north
    Merenptah
    Amenmessu
    Sety II
    Saptah
    Tausret
Dynasty 20 (1186–1069)     Economic decline; weak
    Setnakhte           kings; civil and workers'
    Ramses III–XI      strikes

## Third Intermediate Period: c. 1069–747 B.C.

Dynasty 21 (1069–747)
    Smendes
    Amenemnisu
    Psusennes I
    Amenemope
    Osorkon the elder
    Siamun
    Psuennes II
Dynasty 22 (945–715)     Egypt politically divided
    Sheshonq I
    Osorkon I
    Sheshonq II
    Takelot I
    Osorkon II
    Takelot II
    Sheshonq III
    Pimay
    Sheshonq V
    Osorkon IV
Dynasties 23, 24 (818–715)     Egypt divided among
                                 local rulers

## Late Period: c. 747–332 B.C.

Dynasty 25 (747–656)     Unification of Egypt
                            under Kushite rulers;
    Piy                   cultural revival begins
    Shabaqo
    Shabitqo
    Taharqo
    Tanutamani

Dynasty 26 (664–525)     Saite Dynasty
    Psamtek I
    Nekau II
    Psamtek II
    Apries
    Ahmose II
    Psamtek III
Dynasty 27 (525–404)     Egypt annexed by Persian
    Cambyses          Empire
    Darius I
    Xerxes I
    Artaxerxes I
    Darius II
    Artaxerxes II
Dynasties 28–30     Last native rulers of
    Amyrtaios         Egypt; cultural renaissance
    Nepherites I      but political decline
    Hakor
    Nepherites II
    Nectanebo I
    Teos
    Nectanebo II
Dynasty 31 (343–332)
    Artaxerxes III
    Arses
    Darius III

## Greco-Roman Period: 332 B.C.–A.D. 395

Macedonian Dynasty (332–305)     Alexander the Great rules
                                   until his death in 323,
                                   followed by Macedonian
                                   rulers; Greek becomes
                                   official language of Egypt
Ptolemaic Dynasty (305–30)     Last Ptolemaic ruler,
    Ptolemy I–XV     Cleopatra VII, weds the
                                   Roman Mark Antony,
                                   who is defeated by
                                   Octavian (later Augustus)
Roman Period (30 B.C.–A.D. 395)     Emperor Augustus
                                   appoints himself pharaoh
                                   in 30 B.C.; Egypt declared
                                   imperial estate, rather than
                                   Roman province

# BIBLIOGRAPHY

Aldred, Cyril. *New Kingdom Art in Ancient Egypt During the Eighteenth Dynasty 1570–1320 B.C.,* rev. ed. London, 1961

————. *Jewels of the Pharaohs: Egyptian Jewelry of the Dynastic Period.* London, 1971

————. *Egyptian Art in the Days of the Pharaohs, 3100-320 B.C.* London, 1980

Allen, James P. *Genesis in Egypt: The Philosophy of Ancient Egyptian Creation Accounts,* Yale Egyptological Studies 2. New Haven, 1988

Andrews, Carol. *Egyptian Mummies.* London: British Museum Press; Cambridge, Mass., 1984

————. *Amulets of Ancient Egypt.* London, 1994

Badawy, Alexander. *A History of Egyptian Architecture.* 3 vols. Berkeley, Calif., 1954–68

Bagnall, Roger S. *Egypt in Late Antiquity.* Princeton, 1993

Beadnell, Hugh John Llewellyn. *An Egyptian Oasis.* London, 1909

Bell, B. *The Oldest Records of the Nile Floods.* London, 1970

Belzoni, Giovanni Battista. *Narrative of the Operations and Recent Discoveries in Egypt and Nubia.* London, 1820

Berry, A. C., and R. J. Berry. *Origins and Relations of the Ancient Egyptians.* New York, 1973

Bierbrier, M. L., ed. *Portraits and Masks: Burial Customs in Roman Egypt.* London, 1997

Birch, Samuel. *The Mummies of Deir-el-Bahari.* London, 1881

Bleeker, Claas Jouco. *Hathor and Thoth: Two Key Figures of the Ancient Egyptian Religion.* Leiden, 1973

Boardman, John. *The Greeks Overseas: Their Early Colonies and Trade.,* rev. ed. New York, 1980

Bowman, Alan K. *Egypt After the Pharaohs: 332 B.C.–642 A.D. from Alexander to the Arab Conquest.* Berkeley, Calif., 1986

Brier, Bob. *Egyptian Mummies: Unraveling the Secrets of an Ancient Art.* New York, 1994

————. *The Encyclopedia of Mummies.* New York, 1998

Brooklyn Museum. *Egyptian Sculpture of the Late Period, 700 B.C.–100 A.D.* Brooklyn, 1960

————. *Cleopatra's Egypt: Age of the Ptolemies.* Brooklyn, 1988

Bucaille, Maurice. *Mummies of the Pharaohs: Modern Medical Investigations.* Maurice Bucaille and Alastair D. Pannell, trans. New York, 1989

Clayton, Peter A. *Chronicle of the Pharaohs: The Reign-by-Reign Record of the Rulers and Dynasties of Ancient Egypt.* London, 1994

D'Auria, Sue, Peter Lacovara, and Catherine H. Roehrig, eds. *Mummies and Magic: The Funerary Arts of Ancient Egypt.* Boston, 1988

David, Ann R., and Edmund Tapp, eds. "The History of Mummification," in *The Mummy's Tale: The Scientific and Medical Investigation of Natsef-Amun, Priest in the Temple of Karnak.* New York, 1993

Doxiadis, Euphrosyne. *The Mysterious Fayum Portraits: Faces from Ancient Egypt.* London/New York, 1995

————. "The Mysterious Fayum Portraits" in B. Borg, ed. *Mummien Portrait Chronologie und Kultureller Kontext.* Mainz, 1996

DuQuesne, Terence. *At the Court of Osiris: Book of the Dead Spells.* London, 1994

————. "Seth and the Jackals in Studies Dedicated to the Memory of J. Quaegabeur," *OLA* 83 (1998)

Edgar, Campbell Cowan. *Greco-Egyptian Coffins, Masks and Portraits in Catalogue General des Antiquities Egyptien mes du Musee de Caire.* Cairo, 1905

Edwards, I. E. S., and Alan Wynn Shorter, eds. *A Handbook to the Egyptian Mummies and Coffins Exhibited in the British Museum.* London, 1938

Fakhry, Ahmed. "Bahria and Farafra Oases, Preliminary Reports on New Discoveries," *ASAE* (1938, 1939, 1940)

————. "Die Kapelle aus der Zeit des Apries in der Oase Bahria," in *Archiv für Ägyptische Archaeologie.* Vienna, 1938

————. A Temple of Alexander the Great at Bahria Oasis," *ASAE,* 1940

————. *Bahria Oasis,* 2 vols. Cairo, 1942, 1950

————. *Recent Explorations in the Oases of the Western Desert.* Cairo, 1942

————. *Siwa Oasis: Its History and Antiquities.* Cairo, 1944

————. *The Necropolis of El-Bagawat in Kharga Oasis.* Cairo, 1951

————. *The Oases of Egypt.* vol. 1. Bahria and Farafra Oases. Cairo, 1973

————. *Siwa Oasis,* vol. 2. Bahria and Farafra Oases. Cairo, 1974

Flemming, Stuart, et al. *The Egyptian Mummy Secrets and Science.* Philadelphia, 1980

Garstang, John. *The Burial Customs of the Ancient Egyptians.* London, 1907

Giddy, Lisa L. *Egyptian Oases: Bahariya, Dakhla, Farafra and Kharga During Pharaonic Times.* Warminster, England, 1987

Gray, Peter. "Radiography of Ancient Egyptian Mummies," *Medical Radiology* 43 (1967)

————. "The Radiography of Mummies of Ancient Egyptians," in *Population Biology of the Ancient Egyptians.* London, 1973

Grimm, Gunter. *Die Romischen Mummienmasken aus Ägypten.* Wiesbaden, 1974

Harris, John Richard, ed. *The Legacy of Egypt,* rev. ed. Oxford, 1971

Hassan, F. "Bahria Oasis," in *Encyclopedia of the Archaeology of Ancient Egypt,* Kathryn A. Bard, ed. London/New York, 1999

Hawass, Zahi. "Site Management and Tourism," *Museum International.* New York, 1997

————. *Silent Images: Women in Pharaonic Egypt.* rev. ed. New York, 2000

————. "Roman Mummies Found at Bahariya Oasis," in Jim Sauer, ed. *Festschrift Semitic Museum.* Cambridge, 2000

Hayes, William C. *The Scepter of Egypt: A Background for the Study of the Egyptian Antiquities in The Metropolitan Museum of Art,* rev. ed. New York, 1990

Hornung, Erik. *Conceptions of God in Ancient Egypt: The One and the Many.* John Baines, trans. Ithaca, N.Y., 1982

Ikram, Salima, and Aidan Dodson. *Royal Mummies in the Egyptian Museum.* Cairo, 1997

James, Thomas Garnet Henry. *Pharaoh's People: Scenes from Life in Imperial Egypt.* London, 1984

Kemp, Barry J. *Ancient Egypt: Anatomy of a Civilization.* London/New York, 1989

Leahy, Anthony. ed. *Libya and Egypt c. 1300–750 B.C.* London, 1990

Lewis, Naphtali. *Life in Egypt Under Roman Rule.* Oxford, 1983

————. *Greeks in Ptolemaic Egypt.* Oxford, 1986

Mekhitarian, Arpag. *Egyptian Painting.* Stuart Gilbert, trans. New York, 1979

Morenz, Siegfried. *Egyptian Religion.* Ann E. Keep, trans. London, 1973

Nunn, John F. *Ancient Egyptian Medicine.* London, 1994

O' Connor, David, and David P. Silverman, eds. *Ancient Egyptian Kingship.* Leiden/New York, 1995

Parlasca, K. *Mumienporträts und verwändte Denkmäler.* Wiesbaden, 1966

————. *Repertorio d'Arte dell'Egitto Greco-Roman,* ser. B. Palermo, 1997

Parlasca, Klaus, and Hellmut Seemann. *Mumienporträts und ägyptische Grabkunst aus romischer Zeit: eine Asstellung der Schirn Kunsthalle.* Frankfurt/Munich, 1999

Pestman, Pieter Wilhelm. *Marriage and Matrimonial Property in Ancient Egypt.* Leiden, 1961

Pettigrew, Thomas Joseph. *A History of Egyptian Mummies,* London, 1834

Quirke, Stephen. *The Administration of Egypt in the Late Middle Kingdom: The Hieratic Documents.* New Malden, England, 1990

————. *Ancient Egyptian Religion.* London, 1992

Redford, Donald B. *History and Chronology of the Egyptian Eighteenth Dynasty in Egypt: Seven Studies.* Toronto, 1967

Romano, James F. *Death, Burial and Afterlife in Ancient Egypt.* Pittsburgh, 1990

Schafer, Heinrich. *Principles of Egyptian Art.* Oxford, 1974

Shaw, Ian, and M. Sidarous. "L'Oasis El Bahrieh," in *Congrès Internationale de Géographique.* Cairo, 1926

Shaw, Ian, and Paul T. Nicholson. *The Dictionary of Ancient Egypt.* London/New York, 1995

Silverman, David P. "The Curse of the Curse of the Pharaohs," *Expedition* 29, no. 2 (1987)

————. "Deities and Divinity in Ancient Egypt," in Byron E. Shafer, ed. *Religion in Ancient Egypt: Gods, Myths, and Personal Practice.* Ithaca, N. Y., 1991

Silverman, David P., ed. *Ancient Egypt.* Oxford, 1997

Simpson, W., ed. *Religion and Philosophy in Ancient Egypt.* Yale Egyptological Studies, vol. 3. New Haven, 1989

Smith, Grafton Elliot. *The Royal Mummies.* Cairo, 1912

Spencer, A. Jeffrey. *Death in Ancient Egypt.* London, 1982

Strouhal, Eugen. *Life in Ancient Egypt.* Cambridge/Norman, Okla., 1992

Taylor, John H. *Unwrapping a Mummy: The Life, Death and Embalming of Horemkenesi.* London, 1995

Trigger, Bruce G., et al. *Ancient Egypt: A Social History.* Cambridge/New York, 1993

Troy, Lana. *Patterns of Queenship in Ancient Egyptian Myth and History.* Uppsala, 1986

Uphill, Eric Parrington. *Egyptian Towns and Cities.* Princes Risborough, England, 1988

Van Siclen, Charles Cornell. *Wall Scenes from the Tomb of Amenhotep (Huy) Governor of Bahariya Oasis.* San Antonio, Texas, 1981

Wagner, G. "Les Oasis d'Egypte: à l'époque grècque, romaine et byzantine d'après les documents grecs," *Bibliotheque d'Étude* 100 (1988)

Wente, Edward F. and James E. Harris, eds. *An X-Ray Atlas of the Royal Mummies.* Chicago, 1980

# INDEX

*Page numbers in italics refer to illustrations.*

described, 33–34

excavation of, *30, 31, 34, 36*

Girl mummy, 65, *90, 91, 92, 93,* 95–97

Mummy A, 53, *56,* 57–58

Mummy B, 53, 58–61, *60,* 96

Mummy C, 61–63

mummy conservation at, *39*

mummy placement, in, *32,* 34, 38

plan of, 33, *34,* 36

relation of mummies in, 38, 41

styles of mummies at, *36*

Tomb 55 (Valley of the Golden Mummies), *78, 79, 80, 82,* 83

described, 41–42

*See also* Mr. X (mummy)

Tomb 62 (Valley of the Golden Mummies), 42–44, *145*

Tomb 64 (Valley of the Golden Mummies), 44–45

Tooth infections. *See* abscesses

Toys, as funerary objects, 73

Truitt, Doug, 16

Truitt, Lisa, 16, 17

Tucker, Teri L., 87–89

Tuna el-Gebel, 11, 139, 144

Turin Papyrus, 142

Tutankhamun (ruler), 16, 213

canopic jars of, *134*

coffin, of, 134

and mummification process, 132–34, *143*

and mummy curse, 91–92

tomb discovery of, 27

tomb plan, for, 138

X rays of, 81

Twelfth Dynasty, 104, 183, 212

Twentieth Dynasty, 105, 213

Twenty-fifth Dynasty, 106, 213

Twenty-first Dynasty, 106, 140, 213

Twenty-second Dynasty, 106, 213

Twenty-seventh Dynasty, 107, 213

Twenty-sixth Dynasty, 213

Bahariya Oasis, during, 185

Egypt reunited under, 107

temple dedications, during, 179

tomb group from (El Bawiti), 203–11

and tomb of Bannantiu, *107, 124, 125, 135, 136*

and tomb of Iuf-aa, *130,* 132

*See also* Ahmose II; Ain el-Muftella, Temple of

## U

UCLA, 96

Unas (ruler), *123,* 138, 212

UNESCO, *15*

University of Michigan, 81

University of Pennsylvania, 13, 92

Uraeus, as royal symbol, 57, *62,* 68

*U.S. News and World Report,* 17

Usir. *See* Osiris (god)

## V

Valens (ruler), 110

Valley of the Golden Mummies, *141*

age of mummies in, 68–69, 109

cemetery lifespan, of, 49, 109

coins found in, 78–79

discovery of, 23–25

and DNA testing, 82, 89

excavation team, at, *17*

Greco-Roman style found in, 49

mummy types at, *50,* 53, 69, 157

naming of, 17

and skeletal studies, 87–89

surveys of, 29–31, 47

tombs, in. *See specific* tombs

tomb styles, in, 47–49

views of, *20–21, 22,* 24, *25, 26, 30, 31, 50, 68, 111, 141*

*See also specific* topics

Valley of the Kings (Luxor), *123,* 138

Valley of the Queens (Luxor)

and tomb of Nefertari, *120,* 122, 132, *133, 138*

Vershow (explorer), 113

## W

Wadi el-Ewinat, prehistoric drawings at, 101

Wadi Natrun, 136

Wadjyt (goddess), 206

Wahby, Aiman, 16, *107, 177*

Wah-ibranefer (priest ), 107

Wall paintings, tomb, 46, *47*

funerary texts, in, 67, 121

in New Kingdom, 71–72

in Old Kingdom, 67

provide names of deceased, 83

*See also specific* tombs

*Wedjat*-eye

amulet, as funerary object, 42, 74, *122*

defined, 122

Weeks, Kent, 81

Wente, Edward, 81

Wepwawet (god), 63, 76, 189

Weshet-het (ruler), 106

White Desert, *98–99,* 103, 119

Wigs, Greek style, 61, 63

Wilkinson, John Gardner, 113, 195

Wine, 181

use of, as funerary object, 159, 160, *161*

use of, in sacred rituals, 159

Wine production, 159–67

at Ain el-Rees, 164–66

in Bahariya Oasis, 104, 106, 162–67

and date wine, 162, 166–67

laws regarding, 113

materials used in, 162

process of, 162–63, 165–66

Women, 71

depicted as mourners, 71–72

and dress, 117–19, 187, 206, 208

mummification of (style), *43, 60,* 61, 66

and use of kohl, 73, 76

*Wskh,* defined, 47

## X

X rays, use of, 81, 89

on Mr. X, *86,* 87

## Y

Yemen, *13*

Young, Peter, 96

## Z

Zed-Amun-efankh, tomb of, 185–87, *188,* 206

Zed-Khonsu-efankh (high priest), 93, 107, 113, 193, 194, 195, 205

Zeus. *See* Amun (god)

# ACKNOWLEDGMENTS

THE PREPARATION OF THIS STUDY WAS COMPLETED WITH THE ASSISTANCE OF A NUMBER OF PEOPLE whose cooperation and advice is gratefully acknowledged. First, I wish to acknowledge the supervision and good administration of Ashry Shaker, Director of Antiquities of Bahariya Oasis. Also thanks to the two Mohammeds—the Antiquities Inspectors at Bahariya, Mohammed Tiyab and Mohammed Aiady, who began the first excavation on the site in 1996. I cannot forget to thank the Antiquities Guard of the Temple of Alexander the Great, Abdul Maugoud, who guided us to this discovery. Also I would like to thank Saleh Ali Abdul Maugoud, the owner of El-Beshmo Lodge in the town of El Bawiti, and all of his assistants, especially Sobhy and Ashraf, for their generosity and time to insure that the excavation team and our guests enjoyed a comfortable stay in Bahariya. I am grateful to all of my friends and colleagues with whom I worked on this site, especially Mansour Boriak, Mahmoud Afifi, Tarek el-Awady, Aiman Wahby, Mohammed Ismail, and Noha Abdul Hafiz for their help collecting data and for their support. Without them this book would never be completed. I would like to thank my dear friend Mark Linz, director of the American University in Cairo Press, who was responsible for arranging this book with my publisher, Paul Gottlieb of Harry N. Abrams, Inc. I would also like to thank Barbara Burn, my editor in New York, for all of her work. There is no way I can repay the gracious help of my friends in Egypt, especially Moustafa el-Nagar, Tohfa Handussa, Shafia Bedeer, Michael Jones, and John Swanson for their useful advice. I am also indebted to Aricia Lee for her help in editing the book. I have been fortunate to have the complete support of many friends in the United States, especially Julie Holmes. Last, but not least, I would like to dedicate this book to the soul of the late Dr. Gamal Mokhtar, who supported the work of the late Egyptian archaeologist Ahmed Fakhry and his study of all the Western Desert oases. I am infinitely grateful to Dr. Mokhtar for encouraging me early on to pursue the field of archaeology and then supporting me with his invaluable advice. He will be with us always.

ZAHI HAWASS

# PHOTO CREDITS

*The author and publisher are grateful to the following individuals who have kindly provided photographic material or artwork for use in this book. The photographs not credited below were supplied by the author.*

page 129 top: G. Aldana © J. Paul Getty Trust; page 5, 6, 19, 54 top, 60, 61 left, 62, 65 left, 83 left, 127 bottom, 151: © Marc Deville; page 2–3, 8–9, 20–21, 25, 30 top, 36 top and left, 37, 38 bottom, 41 left, 42, 47 bottom, 49 left, 54 bottom, 55, 63, 64, 65 top right, 67, 68, 69, 70, 72 right,73 left, 76 bottom, 78 top and left, 79, 80, 83 right, 84, 85 top left, middle and bottom, 86 top right, 88, 92, 93, 95 bottom, 96 bottom, 100, 102, 104, 106, 107, 108, 109, 110, 111, 114, 115, 116, 117, 118, 122 right,130, 134, 141, 148, 150, 153, 156, 161 top, 164, top, 167 bottom, 168, 170 top, 179 bottom, 180, 195: © Kenneth Garrett; page 112, 152 bottom, 154 bottom, 164 bottom: © Aricia Lee; page 105, 120, 124, 125, 135, 152 left, 154 top, 173 top, 187 right, 189, 191 right, 202, 205 bottom, 207 top, 210: © Guy Midkiff; page 211: © Rufus Mosley; page 1, 29 top, 35 bottom, 39, 40, 43, 45, 46, 47 top and middle, 51, 54 right, 56, 58, 60 right, 64, 82 bottom, 85 top right, 86 top left and bottom, 87, 90, 95, top, 97, 119 top, 136, 146, 182, 191 left, 196, 198, 199, 200: © Ph. Plailly/Eurelios; page 123 top, 128, 158, 161 top: © Richie Williamson.